Early Texas Women

By Frank M. Johnson

Early Texas Women

Written and published by

Frank M. Johnson

ISBN: 979-8-218-59121-2

Printed by KDP, an Amazon company

Available from:

frankmjohnson.net, Amazon.com, other book outlets

Dedicated to the life and the memory of:

Claudette Denise (Faulkner) Johnson

(1957 – 2022)

"A Special Texas Lady"

Contents

Preface

As a historian, I have researched the history of the United States for many years. My primary focus has been the seventeenth through the nineteenth centuries. Being the sixth generation of my family to live in Texas, I have always had a passion for the incredible history of my native state.

Regardless of how long you have lived in Texas, you quickly realize that this great state has a unique past and that the phrase *"Spirit of Texas"* is more than just a popular expression. This book focuses on how the early women of Texas contributed to that spirit.

I was motivated to write this book because I realized that the historical accounts of women in early Texas were much fewer than those of Texas men. I understand that many issues contributed to this disparity; however, the contributions of these women were just as significant as those of men in shaping the story of Texas.

While examining other publications, I noticed that many of the stories were redundant from one book to another. I realized that some of these stories were too valuable to the history of Texas to be omitted from any book, but I was searching for those unique women whose stories had not been adequately told. My first qualification was that each woman had to have been born or arrived in Texas before the end of 1881 and remained in Texas for most of their life. The second qualification was that they had to be unmistakably independent. Of those women who met the qualifications, many had stories that could not be sufficiently verified, and while they lived incredible lives, I did not feel that I could confidently write their biographies. Many others had fantastic life stories but could not be easily separated from the historical prominence of a father, husband, son, or brother. To resolve the issue, I selected stories that could be told without mentioning any man's name. I am proud to share those stories with you.

2

Acknowledgments

Creating any successful publication requires more than just the ability to put thoughts on paper. It stems from the collective support and contributions of a number of people. In my case, it is a large number of people. First, I would like to acknowledge the love and support of my family and friends. Not only do they lend their encouragement and inspiration, but they also tolerate my failure to return that same love and support during long periods of isolation while I am writing.

Additionally, I extend my thanks to the many friends who dedicate their time and energy to organizations that work tirelessly to preserve the history and heritage of Texas. I particularly appreciate the members of the Montgomery Historical Society for their steadfast support over the years. I would also like to thank the many members of the County Historical Commissions across the state, especially those in Liberty, Angelina, Montgomery, Walker, and Grimes Counties, for their continued support. An inspiration for this book is the many women's heritage organizations, primarily the Daughters of the Republic of Texas, the Daughters of the American Revolution, and the United Daughters of the Confederacy.

I would love to list the many wonderful people who have supported my work, but doing so would require a book of its own. However, I want to express special gratitude to Linda Jamison, the County Chair of the Liberty County Historical Commission, who was instrumental in helping me select some of the women featured in this book.

Introduction

Texas, a vast land of breathtaking vistas, is steeped in a legacy of bold frontiersmen and heroic figures. This remarkable state has inspired countless stories through all forms of media, reflecting its unique heritage. From the arrival of Spanish conquistadors to the current era, Texas has emerged as a powerhouse with one of the largest economies in the world, all while preserving its distinctive spirit and captivating history. The narrative of Texas history has been dominated by men, yet woven into the very fabric of this incredible history are the stories of countless women whose strength, courage, and resourcefulness have shaped the heritage and spirit of Texas.

The disparity between women and men in early Texas is often overlooked. Texas was a dangerous and untamed wilderness, and although women were typically cast in domestic roles, they often found themselves isolated and alone, responsible for caring for and protecting themselves and their children. With little or no access to medical care, childbirth in itself was a heroic feat. The death of a woman and or her child during birth was a common occurrence. Additionally, the threat of violent attacks from native tribes and outlaws loomed in many areas. Women were frequent targets of physical and sexual assault, and you will find in the biographies included in this book that women of early Texas were not afraid of or opposed to using a gun or, in at least one event, a cannon.

The story of women in early Texas dates back more than 13,000 years. Because indigenous tribes did not have a written language, written records first emerged with the arrival of the Spanish in the 16th century. The earliest written accounts of Indigenous women began when the Spanish and French explored present-day Texas in the late 17th century. Women in these tribes often held a higher social status than many early Texas women. While their primary role was that of mothers, they were also valued members of their communities, frequently influencing decision-making and, in rare instances, becoming warriors.

The story of Texas, as we know it today, did not truly begin until the French claimed an area of present-day Texas in 1685. The threat of the French entering the area claimed by the Spanish to be a part of New Spain forced the Spanish to explore Texas, and Domingo Terán de los Ríos was appointed the first governor of the newly created Provincia de Tejas (Province of Texas) on January 23, 1691. Among the earliest European settlers in Texas was a group that came from the Canary Islands and arrived at the presidio of San Antonio de Bexar on March 9, 1731. Because the Canary Islands were considered to be a part of Spain, these families held special privileges in New Spain. The first biography in this book, Maria del Carmen Calvillo, was a descendant of one of those families. The second of the biographies, Angelina, was a native of the Hasinai tribes of East Texas, and the third biography was Jane Wilkinson Long, one of the earliest Anglo women in Texas. I did not choose these women because of their ethnicity but rather their incredible contribution to the heritage, history, and spirit of Texas.

When Mexico won its independence from Spain in 1821, the lives of women in Mexican Texas made gradual changes. One crucial aspect that did not change was the advantages given to women under Spanish law, often called *"Castilian Law."* These laws were essential to the rights of women concerning property and legal standing, and their influence continued into the days of the Republic of Texas.

No longer under Spanish rule, the privileged social status of women with pure Spanish blood not only diminished but created a serious resentment between the Spanish Peninsulares and the Criollos born in Mexico. Adding to the resentment was a flood of Anglos immigrating to Mexican Texas. With the arrival of the ever-growing Anglo population came the issue of slavery. Contrary to popular belief, the Mexican Constitution adopted in 1824 did not explicitly abolish slavery, and in fact, it would have conflicted with existing contracts between the Mexican Government and Empresarios, who were bringing settlers to Texas. Mexican President Vicente Guerrero presented a proclamation banning the practice in 1829, but because the powers of the President were subordinate to the Legislative Branch, the proclamation was never put into force, and some historians believe that the issuance of the declaration contributed to Guerro's removal from office and execution.

Slavery, having been a stain on the history of the United States, remained a stain on the history of Texas until it was abolished by the 13th amendment to the U.S. Constitution when it was ratified on December 18, 1865. Being considered property by law and their owner, the stories of these women were seldom recorded and were most often handed down by word of mouth.

Their accounts were usually given years after they were freed from the bonds of slavery, leaving little evidence to corroborate them. Thus, the life stories of thousands of black women have been excluded from the recorded history of Texas, and their legacy has been lost to time.

The lives of Native American women in Mexican Texas were little changed for those in tribes like the Caddo Confederation, who were basically farmers, but for the nomad tribes such as the Apache, Kiowa, and Comanche, things grew steadily worse as their lands were encroached upon by the influx of settlers.

A new group of immigrants began to arrive in Texas under Mexican rule. A German man named Johann Friedrich Ernst arrived in Mexican Texas on March 9, 1831, and settled near present-day Industry, Texas. His letters to a friend back home told of the beauty and opportunities available in Texas and were widely published in Germany. His actions triggered a movement, causing more than 7,000 Germans to immigrate to Texas by 1847.

Chapter 2 - Mexican Texas (1821 – 1836), features the biographies of three remarkable women. First is Sarah Ann Groce Wharton, the daughter of the wealthiest man in Mexican Texas. Next is Margaret Leatherbury Hallett, who sailed with her husband from Baltimore, Maryland, to Mexico and later became a successful businesswoman near the town of Hallettsville, which was named in her honor. The final biography is of Sarah Jane Newman, also known as *"Sally Scull,"* who earned the title *"The Scariest Siren in Texas."* Their stories illustrate the broad range of backgrounds and accomplishments of the women who have contributed to the spirit of Texas.

Chapter 3 – The Republic of Texas (1836 – 1845) begins with the inevitable clash between early Texas settlers and the increasingly autocratic Mexican government. This era of social unrest and the struggles to form a new nation reveals the vital roles played by the incredible women of early Texas and includes the biographies of 5 amazing women who have left an indelible mark on the history, heritage, and spirit of Texas. The first biography is of Susanna Wilkerson Dickinson, a survivor of the Alamo who transformed her tragedy into triumph. Following her story is Pamelia Dickinson Mann, a legendary figure who gained high social standing and respect as a businesswoman despite her unusual notoriety. Next, we have Margaret Robertson Wright, who secretly aided soldiers who were escaping the Goliad

Massacre and later became a successful rancher despite a toxic marriage. The fourth biography is of Rosalie von Roeder Kleberg, a German immigrant who courageously survived the challenges of a harsh Texas frontier. The last biography is of Angelina Belle Peyton Eberly, a courageous Texas patriot who once used a cannon to demonstrate her forcefulness. Each in their own way, these women made their mark on Texas history.

Chapter 4 – The State of Texas (1841 – 1865). Despite initial resistance rooted in fears of renewed conflict with Mexico, the desire of Texans for annexation ultimately prevailed, transforming the Republic of Texas into the 28th U.S. State. This transition, however, ushered in a period of change and hardship, marked by the Mexican-American War, intensified struggles for Native American populations, and the looming shadow of the Civil War, which would test the resilience of Texan women in ways that would forever shape the identity of Texas. This chapter includes the biographies of 7 early Texas women who profoundly influenced the culture and spirit of Texas. The first of these biographies is that of Sophia Suttenfield Porter, a true Southern Belle who managed her plantation on the Red River. Then, the biography of Cynthia Ann Parker, who was captured by Comanches as a child, later rescued against her will, and spent the rest of her life yearning to return to the Comanche people. A third biography is of Mary Ann Adams Maverick, a true Texas patriot. Next is the biography of Sarah Horton Cockrell, who was instrumental in the founding and development of Dallas. Next, the fifth biography is of Betty Wilhelmine Holekamp, an important figure in German culture in early Texas. The sixth biography is of Sarah Ridge Pix, a woman of Cherokee descent; she was a prominent figure in the history of Galveston and Chambers County. The final biography of the chapter is of Elizabeth "Bettie" Munn Gay, a social activist and champion of women's rights.

Chapter 5 - The Texas Frontier (1865 – 1890) is the story of a tumultuous era defined by relentless expansion, violent conflict, and the stark realities of survival. While romanticized notions of the "Wild West" often overshadow the brutal truth, this period was a complex struggle for control, marked by the displacement of Native Americans, the rise of the cattle industry, and the hard-won establishment of law and order. Despite the inherent dangers and hardships, the era's enduring legacy is one of resilience and transformation. This chapter includes the incredible biographies of three "Cattle Queens," Margaret Heffernan Borland, Henrietta Chamberlain King, and Elizabeth

"*Lizzie*" Johnson Williams. It also contains the biographies of Mary Ann "*Molly*" Dyer Goodnight, savior of the Southern Plains Buffalo, Anna Mebus Martin, the first woman bank president in Texas, and Charlotte Tompkins Thurmond "*Lottie Deno,*" the "*Poker Queen,*" whose life was the inspiration for the character "*Miss Kitty*" in the television series "*Gunsmoke.*"

The final Chapter, "*The Preservationists,*" is dedicated to the many women of early Texas who tirelessly and passionately endeavored to preserve the history of Texas. Three examples are the biographies of Cornelia Branch Stone, Adina Emilia De Zavala, and Clara Driscoll, shining examples of the true "*Spirit of Texas.*"

The exceptional women featured in this book are just a glimpse of the many who have profoundly impacted the history, heritage, and spirit of Texas. Tragically, numerous stories of remarkable women have gone unheard and faded into obscurity. Yet, their enduring legacies continue to resonate throughout Texas, reminding us of the vital role women have played in shaping our collective story. Let us celebrate not only those we recognize but also the countless others whose contributions deserve to be remembered.

Chapter 1 - Spanish Texas
(1535 – 1821)

"The Romance and Tragedy of Pioneer Life" William Ludwell (Ludlow) Sheppard, 1883, public domain-US

To understand the unique and extraordinary character of women in Spanish Texas, it is essential to recognize the harsh environment in which they lived. New Spain was marked by rugged terrain, extreme climate, and countless predators and hazards. It's difficult to fully appreciate the immense struggles of daily life during that time. These remarkable women served as mothers, wives, missionaries, businesswomen, and fighters. Their ability to persevere and rise above adversity highlights their historical significance. The courageous efforts of these women embody the very essence of the "Spirit of Texas."

Some eighty-eight years before the founding of the Jamestown Colony on the Atlantic coast of North America, Spanish conquistador Hernán Cortés arrived on the Yucatán Peninsula of present-day Mexico in 1519, claiming the area for Spain. Following two years of brutal war, Cortés toppled the Aztec city of Tenochtitlan, thus ending Aztec rule, and colonization of the area began. In 1535, the Spanish Crown officially established the Viceroyalty of New Spain.

Although there is no precise date on which the Spanish Provinces of Coahuila and Texas were actually created, Domingo Terán de los Ríos was appointed the first governor of the newly created Provincia de Tejas (Province of Texas) on January 23, 1691. This is the date when the story of Texas truly begins.[1]

A particular "*Caste*," or social class, was established when settlement began in New Spain. Social class was determined by a person's birth rather than wealth or accomplishments. Because there were so few people in the new colony, social class was less rigid than that of Spain, but it was still an essential part of the new culture. The Spanish colonial government divided the population into these social classes:[2]

> **Peninsulares:** These were people born in Spain and held the highest social status.
>
> **Creoles (Criollos):** These were people born in the Americas to Spanish parents and held the 2nd highest rank in the class.
>
> **Mestizos:** These were people of mixed Spanish and Native American ancestry and held the 3rd highest rank.
>
> **Mulattos:** These were people of mixed Spanish and African ancestry and were of lower social status than mestizos.
>
> **Slaves:** These were people who were owned by other people. They were of the lowest social status.

The importance of social class meant that there were rare occasions when some women held a higher status than certain men. However, this does not imply the existence of gender equality. Under Spanish law, women in New Spain enjoyed more rights than women in many other countries; still, within the same levels of the social hierarchy, men consistently occupied a higher position. Even in the newly acquired territory, women were assigned specific roles.

In the late 17th century, incursions by French explorers created an alarming problem for the Spanish Crown and the leadership of New Spain. This was the catalyst for Spanish exploration into the area of New Spain that we now know as Texas. Four expeditions between 1686 and 1689 opened the door to the settlement of Texas. The Spanish settlement model was establishing a mission guarded by a Presidio (fort). Although Corpus Christi de la Ysleta del Sur, established near El Paso in 1682, was the first Spanish Mission north of the Rio Grande River, the area was not considered a part of Texas at that time[3]. The first Spanish mission in Provincia de Tejas, San Francisco de los Tejas, was established in present-day Houston County, Texas, in 1690 but housed only priests and soldiers.[4] After the failure of the mission, similar missions were created as far east as Natchitoches Parish, Louisiana. There, a mission, San Miguel de Cuellar de los Adaes, and a presidio, Nuestra Señora del Pilar de Los Adaes, was established and served as the capital of Provincia de Tejas from 1729 to 1770. All of the Spanish Missions in Northeast Texas and Western Louisiana were eventually abandoned in favor of relocation to San Antonio, which became the Capitol of Provincia de Tejas in 1773.[5]

Although the stories of many of the magnificent women in Spanish Texas have been lost to time, a group of women arriving from the Canary Islands began to make their mark on the culture and history of Texas. Sometime before June 1730, the King of Spain suggested the resettlement of families from the Canary Islands in New Spain. It is unclear how many of these families arrived in Texas. It is believed that fifty-six former Canary Islanders arrived in San Fernando de Béxar's villa on March 9, 1731. Because the Canary Islands were considered to be a part of Spain, these immigrants were given a higher social status than those born in New Spain. Despite their noble status, women had to cook, clean, plant crops, tend to livestock, make clothes, raise children, and defend themselves and their children from wild animals and attacks from native tribes. These women and their descendants became the very definition of womanhood in early Texas.

The Spanish reign over Texas ended when the Treaty of Córdoba was signed on August 24, 1821. Most of the written accounts of women in early Texas prior to that date concerned women of Spanish descent. There are only a few narratives concerning slaves, mulattos, and women of indigenous tribes. Sadly, many stories were never written at all, but the absence of written documentation does not diminish the significance of these women's contributions to the culture and history of Texas.

The first Anglo child born in Spanish Texas was likely Helena (Dill) Berryman in 1804. Several more Anglo women entered Spanish Texas during the filibustering campaigns between 1812 and 1821, but of these, only the history of Jane Herbert Wilkinson Long is well documented. Since the Spanish reign ended in 1821, most historical accounts of Anglo women in Texas did not begin to appear until the Mexican era (1821-1836).

This chapter presents the biographies of some remarkable women who played a significant role in shaping the history of Spanish Texas. Their ethnic origins, while distinct, are not the defining feature of their inclusion. These women were selected for their determination and their extraordinary achievements. Their stories serve as a testament to courage, innovation, and resilience. They are an undeniable part of the rich heritage and history of Texas.

Maria del Carmen Calvillo
(1765–1856)

The "Spirit of Texas" embodies a wild, untamed force that resists simple categorization. It lives in the hearts and minds of those who reflect the state's rugged individualism, vibrant culture, and rich, tumultuous history. Among the remarkable figures representing the Texas spirit is Maria del Carmen Calvillo, a woman whose name resonates through time, symbolizing the indomitable spirit that shaped this legendary land. In the vast expanse of Provincia de Tejas, where men traditionally held power, Maria Calvillo forged her own destiny, becoming a legend embedded in the very soil. She inherited a sprawling ranching empire and was determined not just to maintain it, but to expand its reach, acquiring acres of land with an ambition rarely displayed by women of her time. In the early days of Texas, Maria Calvillo displayed a courage equal to that of the bravest man, while blazing her own trail in history.

Courtesy of the University of Texas at San Antonio, Special Collections, Image is in the Public Doman

Maria del Carmen Calvillo was born on July 9, 1765, in La Villa de San Fernando de Béxar, Provincia de Tejas, Nueva España (present-day San Antonio). She was the eldest child of Ignacio (also spelled Ygnacio) Francisco Xavier and Antonia Arocha Calvillo. Her father was a well-known rancher,

Procurador General (councilman), and Alcalde (mayor) of San Fernando de Béxar. Maria's mother, María Antonia de Arocha, descended from a family of Canary Islanders, holding a higher social status than Spaniards born in New Spain. Church records indicate that Ignacio Calvillo and Antonia Arocha were married in 1760. Her family's social status likely contributed to Ignacio's success as a rancher and local politician.

In the 18th century, the province of Tejas was a brutal environment. The village of San Fernando de Béxar was sparsely populated but had several Spanish Missions, a presidio (fort), and an irrigation system. It served as the Capital of the province of Tejas from 1773 until the overthrow of the Spanish Government in 1821. It is believed that Ignacio Calvillo started his career raising cattle on his brother-in-law's land. It is known that Calvillo moved with his family to land that he leased. He later purchased this ranch known as the El Paso de las Mujeres or Nuestra Señora de las Mujeres. The ranch was located near present-day Floresville in Wilson County and near a ranch known as Rancho de las Cabras (goat ranch), which was maintained by the Mission San Francisco de la Espada. It is unknown when Ignacio Calvillo acquired the Rancho de las Cabras, but he applied for title to the land in 1809.

Maria Calvillo's accomplishments began while learning the ranching business from his father, sharpening his skills with a horse, a rope, and a gun. She was married to Juan Gavino de la Trinidad Delgado around 1781. During their marriage, Maria and Juan had two sons: Juan Bautista, born in 1782, and José Anacleto, born in 1784. Both children died in infancy. Later, the couple adopted three children: Juan José, María Concepción Gortari, and Antonio Durán. After thirty years of marriage, Maria's life entered a period of difficult trials. During the years of 1811 through 1814, her husband Juan joined the revolutionary movement involved with the overthrow of the Spanish Government. His actions caused him to be declared an enemy of the Crown. Maria separated from her husband sometime during that period and maintained all claims to his father's land. In 1814, Maria's father was killed during an apparent raid by Lipon Apaches. When Spanish authorities investigated the murder, one witness claimed that Ingacio's grandson, Ignacio Casanova, was among the attackers.

Being the oldest child, Maria inherited his father's land. She formally petitioned the Mexican government for a title on August 28, 1828, which was granted the next month. In 1833, another three leagues of land (more than 13,000 acres) were placed under her control. She later added a granary, a sugar mill, and an irrigation system to her property. Maria worked long and hard days taking care of her ranch. It was said that she could ride, rope, and shoot as well as any man. She sometimes gave tribute to hostile native tribes by giving them beef in exchange for protecting her property, and even though some of her neighbors were angered by her actions, they did not dare to cross her. More impressive than her accomplishments was that she managed her operation almost single-handedly.

Maria del Carmen Calvillo died on January 15, 1856. Currently, there is no record of her burial. She left her property to María Concepción Gortari and Antonio Durán, her adopted daughter and son. The ride to her magnificent life traveled through many dark canyons of suffering and grief. The death of two small sons and the vicious murder of her father had to have taken its toll. Years of being trapped in the middle of a savage conflict between residents and the Spanish Army and knowing that her husband had contributed to the hostilities added to her troubles. The Battle of Medina, the bloodiest battle in Texas history, occurred less than 30 miles from her property. Maria managed to rise above all the adversity. According to local folklore, Maria can sometimes be seen riding through the countryside on a great white horse, though no eyewitness has been named. Even if there is no daring cowgirl riding hard across the prairie, the spirit of Maria del Carmen Calvillo rides through the heart of Texas.

Angelina

Of the 254 counties in Texas, only one is named for a woman. Her Spanish name was simply Angelina. The epic story of this Hasinai woman influenced early Texas culture so much that her memory has survived the course of time. Because there is little recorded history about her, some contend that her story is a myth. While we may never know the full truth, the significance of the name Angelina and her legacy are undeniable.

It is said that Angelina was from the Hasinai tribes of East Texas, a large Confederation of the Caddo Nation. Some of the more prominent tribes within the Hasinai Confederation were the Hainai, Nabedache, Neche, and Nacogdoche. Angelina's exact tribe is unknown. Her birthdate is assumed to be prior to 1790. A Spanish Priest, Father Damián Massanet, is given credit for naming her Angelina. This is highly possible since Father Massanet helped establish the San Francisco de los Tejas Mission in 1690 and was known to have ministered to the Hasinai tribe.[6] Angelina likely learned to speak Spanish during that period.

A French chronicler, André Joseph Pénicaut, claimed that on a trip with Louis Juchereau de St. Denis through the Hasinai village, he encountered a woman named Angelique, who had been baptized by Spanish priests and spoke Spanish. The dates recorded in his chronicles did not match the dates of the actual events, so the reliability of his claim is suspect or might have been a secondhand account.[7] Many historians contend that there is at least some credible information in his story.

A more credible account came from another Frenchman named François Simars de Bellisle. His ship was bound for Louisiana in 1719 but got lost and ran aground near Galveston Bay. After all of his shipmates died of disease or exposure, he found himself stranded in East Texas, captured by members of the Atákapa tribe, and treated as a slave. Eventually, he managed to get a written message to members of the neighboring Bidai tribe, who in turn passed the message to the Hasinai. Members of the Hasinai tribe delivered the message to Louis Juchereau de St. Denis at Fort Saint-Jean-Baptiste in Natchitoches, Louisiana. At the request of St. Denis, Hasinai men were sent to rescue Bellisle and arrived at the Hasinai in late 1720. After his rescue, Bellisle spent several months among the Hasinai people. There, he met a young widow named Angelique, who spoke about her time with the Spanish people. Bellisle was impressed by her kindness. He claimed that he was later guided by her sons to Natchitoches, where he arrived on February 10, 1721.[8] His account of his time with the Hasinai contributes to the validity of the story of Angelina.

Spanish accounts which mention Angelina are the most credible. On April 27, 1716, Spanish officer Domingo Ramón led an expedition from Coahuila into Spanish Texas. The entourage of seventy-five people, including the newly appointed commissary office Louis Juchereau de St. Denis, Isidro Félix de Espinosa, soldiers, priests, friars, and civilians. Espinosa kept a diary of the activities of the expedition. Upon arriving at the Hasinai village, an entry in his diary is particularly telling when he states: "*Having recourse to a learned Indian woman of this tribe, reared in Coahuila, we gave them to understand, as best we could, the object of our coming.*"[9] While he did not mention Angelina by name, he did state that she was a member of that tribe.

On December 9, 1716, Martín de Alarcón was appointed governor of the Province of Texas. In 1718 and 1719, he conducted expeditions in Texas to supply existing Spanish missions and establish new ones. A diary of his expedition was written by Fray Francisco Céliz. He reported that during a visit to an East Texas mission, Alarcón participated in the baptism of three Native Americans and commented that "*the governor proceeded to distribute clothing to all the family of those baptized, among whom is found the sagacious Indian woman interpreter.*"[10] Here again, the name Angelina was never mentioned, still, it is likely that Alarcón was referring to her.

During Marqués de San Miguel de Aguayo's expedition to East Texas in 1721, Chaplain Juan Antonio de la Peña mentioned that a woman named Angelina, who had grown up in Coahuila, served as a translator between Aguayo and Hasinai Chiefs because she spoke both Castilian and the language of the Tejas.[11] This was probably the last recorded mention of Angelina.

So, who is that sagacious Indian woman interpreter that so many remember as Angelina? Whether real or mythical, governors, priests, soldiers, and explorers were enthralled by Angelina. There was Angelina's village, Angelina's River, Angelina County, and even Angelina National Forest. The answers are lost in time, but that mystique is embedded in our heritage and culture. A worthy contribution to the *"Spirit of Texas."*

Jane Herbert Wilkinson Long
(1798–1880)

Jane Herbert Wilkinson Long
Courtesy of the
Daughters of the Republic of Texas
Image is in the public domain

The arrival of Anglo-Americans in Texas began during the era of the filibusters. These individuals attempted to establish independent republics in Texas during Spanish and then Mexican rule. One of the last and possibly the best-known filibusters was a man named James Long. While his endeavors ended in failure and his tragic death, the remarkable accomplishments of his wife, Jane Herbert Wilkinson Long, remain remarkable testaments to the resilience and dedication of women in early Texas. She was born Jane Herbert Wilkinson in Charles County, Maryland, on July 23, 1798, and was the 10th child of Captain William Mackall and Anne Herbert Dent Wilkinson.[12] After her father died in 1799, her mother moved the family to Mississippi. When his mother died in 1813, Jane went to live with her older sister Barbara and her husband, Alexander Calvit, at Propinquity Plantation near Natchez, Mississippi. There, she met a doctor from Virginia named James Long, and they were married on May 14, 1815.[13] After the couple married, James practiced medicine in Port Gibson, Mississippi. Her first child, a daughter named Ann, was born there on November 26, 1816.[14]

As early as the 1790s, Americans began developing a strong interest in the vast lands and possibilities of wealth in Spanish Texas. This interest triggered a series of unlawful expeditions into Spanish Texas. Among the earliest of these expeditions were led by Phillip Nolan. His endeavors were partially organized and financed by General James Wilkinson, the uncle of Jane Long. It is undetermined how much influence General Wilkinson had on Dr. James Long, but he and his wife Jane were dedicated to the prospects in Texas. On February 22, 1819, the United States of America signed a treaty with Spain called the Adams-Onís Treaty.[15] The agreement ceded Spain's claims of

Florida to the United States and set the border between Spanish Texas and the United States along the Sabine River. People in Natchez, Mississippi, were enraged by the Treaty and began organizing an expedition into Spanish Texas. Because the expedition's goal was to seize land from Spain and establish a republic, the action, by definition, was a filibuster.

On June 8, 1819, an advance force of the expedition crossed the Sabine River. The commander, James Long, arrived at Nacogdoches, Texas, with additional men on June 22.[16] Jane could not follow her husband to Texas because their second daughter, Rebecca, was born on June 16, 1819.[17] As soon as she was able, Jane traveled with his two daughters and a slave girl named Kian to Alexandria, Louisiana, where his sister and brother-in-law were living. After a brief illness, Jane left her two daughters with them while traveling to Texas with Kian.[18] They arrived at Nacogdoches in August 1819.

Before Jane's arrival, the expedition had declared the independence of Texas, established a Supreme Council, and a provisional government. James Long hoped to receive support and supplies from the infamous pirate Jean Laffite on Galveston Island, but no support was given. When Spanish officials learned of Long's actions, Governor Antonio María Martínez ordered Colonel Ignacio Pérez, with more than 500 men, to drive Long out of Texas. He reached Nacogdoches on October 28, 1819, and within a month, had driven all of the men of the expedition across the Sabine River. Both James and Jane Long escaped capture. When Jane returned to Alexandria, Louisiana, she learned that little Rebecca had died.[19]

In 1820, James Long traveled to New Orleans to seek support for another expedition into Spanish Texas. With the aid of José Félix Trespalacios, Benjamin R. Milam, and José Bernardo Gutiérrez de Lara, James was able to reinvigorate his Supreme Council and establish a headquarters called Fort Las Casas on the Bolivar Peninsula of Texas. His wife Jane, daughter Ann, and his slave girl Kian followed him to Bolivar. Due to the absence of proper pay and supplies, many of his men abandoned the expedition. On September 19, 1821, James Long and 52 men left Bolivar to capture the town of La Bahía (present-day Goliad). The town fell with little resistance on October 4, 1821.

On October 8, 1821, Long and his men were captured by the forces of Ignacio Pérez and taken to prison in San Antonio. Long was transferred to Nuevo León and later to Mexico City, where he attempted to plead his case before Agustín de Iturbide. On April 8, 1822, James was shot and killed by a guard. While the shooting was said to be an accident, there was evidence that the guard was hired to kill him by José Félix Trespalacios, who had become a Colonel in the Mexican Cavalry.[20]

Still waiting on the Bolivar Peninsula, Jane Long knew nothing of her husband's fate. The few citizens who had remained at Fort Las Casas soon left due to the lack of supplies. Jane, her daughter Ann, and slave Kian were left alone on Bolivar Island and often hungry. Her story tells that she once fired a cannon to give local natives the impression that the fort was occupied. To complicate her situation further, Jane was pregnant, and on December 21, 1821, she gave birth to a little girl whom she named Mary James Long.[21] The winter of 1822 was brutal on the Bolivar Peninsula, but Jane was still determined to wait for the return of her beloved husband. Soon, her situation turned from bad to grave. Near starving and concerned about her infant child, she agreed to travel with a passing immigrant family to an area near the mouth of the San Jacinto River where she could get food and shelter. Months later, Jane learned that her husband had been killed. Eventually, she petitioned her husband's former associate and newly appointed governor, José Félix Trespalacios, for a pension. She claimed that her husband's efforts contributed to Mexican independence, but her claims were denied. Indigent with no place to turn, Jane returned to her family in Mississippi, where his youngest daughter, Mary James Long, died in 1824.[22]

Still clinging to the memories of her deceased husband and the dreams that they shared about the land that he gave his life for, Jane yearned to return to Texas. On April 30, 1827, Jane obtained a sitio of land (4,428 acres) in empresario Stephen F. Austin's colony in Mexican Texas, near present-day Fort Bend County. On May 1, 1827, she obtained a labor of land (177 acres) further north in the colony.[23] When Jane arrived in Texas, it was unclear whether she lived on her smaller parcel of land or the San Felipe de Austin settlement. Little is known about her time there. In April 1830, Jane took her daughter Ann to Mississippi to be educated. On January 18, 1831, Ann married James Edward Winston in Warren County, Mississippi. She was pregnant with her first child when her husband died in 1832. After his death, Jane and Ann returned to Texas, where Jane operated a boarding house in Brazoria. In 1836, citizens of Texas revolted against the Mexican Government. As the Mexican Army entered Texas, Jane and most of the families of Texas fled toward the Louisiana border in a movement known as the "runaway scrape." The families returned after Texas won its independence at the Battle of San Jacinto. When Jane returned, she moved to her land in Fort Bend County. After arriving in Fort Bend County, Jane sold a portion of his land, which developers used to establish the City of Richmond. She started another boarding house there in 1837. Jane also bought and sold land, raised cattle, and grew cotton. She died at the age of 82 on December 30, 1880, and was buried in Morton Cemetery, Richmond, Texas.[24] Her last remaining child, Ann, preceded her in death on June 1, 1870, and is also buried in Morton Cemetery.

Jane Long showed remarkable resolve throughout a life of constant adversity. She was an orphan at 15, a widow at 23, and gave birth to a child in the wilderness with virtually no assistance at age 24. Her love and devotion to her husband during their short marriage was incredible. For many years, she was called the "mother of Texas" because, at the time, it was believed that he had given birth to the first Anglo-American child in Texas. She is just as easily deserving of the title for her unmatched devotion to Texas and its people. She was a patriot, a businesswoman, and a friend to all who knew her. Throughout her remarkable 82 years, Jane's belief in Texas remained steadfast.

Chapter 2 - Mexican Texas
(1821 – 1836)

In Texas, the period between Mexican Independence in 1821 and Texas Independence in 1836 was one of dramatic change and escalating tensions. In those fifteen years, Mexico was ruled by one monarch and four presidents. The rights and privileges of women in Texas decreased with each change of leadership. The first ruler, Agustín de Iturbide, was regarded as a champion of independence during the Mexican Revolution for his brilliant role as a military leader. After Mexico was declared an independent empire, Iturbide was appointed President by a 36-member junta, and on May 19, 1822, was proclaimed Agustín I, Emperor of Mexico. He called for equality between the Criollos and Peninsulares. With this, the privileges and protections awarded to women of pure Spanish heritage were greatly diminished, and the resentment between the two classes increased. Overall, the societal structure of Mexican Texas became more patriarchal. The most eventful change during Iturbide's reign was his approval of Stephen F. Austin's plan to bring 300 families to the Mexican province of Texas. The plan allowed settlers to bring slaves with them. Soon, the number of Anglo-Americans and their slaves would grow exponentially. Due to widespread opposition to his rule, Iturbide abdicated his throne on March 19, 1823.

Guadalupe Victoria became President of the fragile First Republic of Mexico on October 10, 1824. During his Presidency, the Constitution of 1824 was ratified. It was the first step toward stability during a time of turmoil. It leaned toward a strong legislature and limited the powers of the President. In addition, it eliminated the special legal status held by some indigenous communities previously held as wards of the Crown of Spain. The official religion of Mexico was Catholicism. The Constitution of 1824 was silent on the subject of slavery. Colonists were given a degree of self-government, which allowed them some control over local affairs.

Vicente Ramón Guerrero was recognized as President on April 1, 1829. He was one of the most controversial presidents of the era. On September 15, 1829, he issued what became known as the "Guerrero Decree," which, with the exception of the Isthmus of Tehuantepec, abolished slavery throughout the Republic of Mexico. The decree was likely an attempt to slow immigration into Texas but would have been in violation of the colonization laws. With the limited powers of the Presidency and because it was not approved by the legislature, the decree had no merit and was never enacted. It was one of the actions that caused a revolt, leading him to be replaced by Anastacio Bustamante. On February 14, 1831, Guerrero was executed by a firing squad.

Anastacio Bustamante was serving as President of Mexico when the Law of April 6, 1830, was enacted. The law succeeded in limiting immigration from the United States and restricting the rights of the colonists given them under the Constitution of 1824. It became the driving force behind the Texas Revolution.

The fourth President of the Republic of Mexico was Antonio López de Santa Anna. Although he envisioned himself as the Napolean of the West, he will be best remembered in history as a ruthless tyrant. He was elected President of the Republic of Mexico in 1833 as a liberal, but in 1834, he emerged as the dictator of an autocratic centralist government with no regard for law. For two years, Santa Anna waged a cruel war of oppression against everyone that challenged his authority. His reign of terror ended with his capture by the Texas Army at the Battle of San Jacinto.

The years of turmoil under Mexican rule could not distract women from the grim realities of life in Texas. It was still a harsh, untamed wilderness. Whether they were Mexican, Caucasian, French, or members of an indigenous tribe, women faced similar hardships. A significant challenge for all women was an environment of soaring heat to bone-chilling cold accompanied by storms, floods, animal attacks, and insect bites, which often carried diseases such as yellow fever. The problem of safely preparing and storing food, accompanied by the shortage of clean drinking water, often caused cholera. Outbreaks of smallpox and measles were also common. Settling in Texas meant back-breaking work, from tending crops and livestock to an array of domestic duties. Women were forced to be alert and vigilant for their own safety and the safety of their children. One hardship unique to women was the incredible task of giving birth to a child in the wilderness. Death of a woman or her newborn was common during childbirth. Like any area of lawlessness, women during that era of Texas were often subjected to physical or sexual abuse. Surviving daily life was usually an astounding achievement.

Preserving the history of these remarkable women is a challenging task. Few records of the deeds and accomplishments of these pioneering women were saved during the period of Texas under, Mexican rule and many stories of historic importance have been lost forever. Fortunately, there are still some great stories about the women of this period. The profiles of these women range from angels to outlaws and all types between. Regardless of their deeds or personalities, they were all threads of the fabric that created Texas.

Sarah Ann Groce Wharton
(1810–1878)

Most stories about women in Mexican Texas include tales of struggles and hardships in an untamed wilderness. The story of Sarah Ann (Groce) Wharton was significantly different. Although she lived much of her life in relatively elegant surroundings, she encountered trials that required tremendous courage and unabated commitment.

Sarah Ann Groce was born in Lincoln County, Georgia, in 1810. She was the second child of Mary Ann Waller Groce and Jared Ellison Groce II. Her father was likely the wealthiest settler in the history of Mexican Texas. An older brother, Leonard Waller Groce, was born September 27, 1805, and a younger brother, Jared Ellison Groce III, was born September 5, 1812. Both brothers would later become wealthy plantation owners in Texas.

After the death of his wife Mary Ann, Jared Groce, married his wife's sister, Anna Chiles Waller and moved his family to an area near Mobile, Alabama. There, he established a settlement that he called Fort Groce. Records about Jared's second marriage are sketchy at best. Some records show that the couple had two sons, Waller William, who died as an infant and Edwin who supposedly drowned in the Brazos River in or about 1830. Anna Chiles Groce died around March 1818.

In 1821, Jared Groce received several leagues (4,428 acres) of land in Stephen F. Austin's original colony. Traveling from Alabama, Jared and his sons, along with more than 50 covered wagons, all his livestock, and all of his slaves, reached New Orleans in December 1821.[25] His daughter Sarah Ann had been sent to boarding school in Nashville, Tennessee, in 1818. The caravan reached the Brazos River in Mexican Texas in January 1822.[26] Jared chose a site about 4 miles south of present-day Hempstead, Texas, for his homesite. Upon its completion, he named his new home "Bernardo."

William Harris Wharton, an attorney from Nashville, Tennessee, visited Bernardo Plantation in 1827. After meeting Sarah Ann Groce, a courtship quickly developed. William and Sarah were married at Bernardo Plantation on December 5, 1827. After the marriage, the couple moved to Nashville, Tennessee. Their only son, John Austin Wharton, was born there on July 3, 1828. As an enticement to return and stay in Texas, Jared Groce gave the couple 5 leagues of land in Brazoria County, Texas. After receiving such a generous gift, William quickly returned with his family to Texas. The couple named their new plantation "Eagle Island." Soon after, they built an elaborate home fashioned after a mansion in Mobile, Alabama. It was located on Oyster Creek, approximately twelve miles from the Gulf of Mexico.

In the early 1830s, Sarah Ann Wharton was nearing the turning point of what must have seemed to be a fairy tale life, but soon, she faced events that would test the resolve of any woman. For reasons unknown, William and Sarah adopted Anne Cleveland, whose mother died on the trip from New Orleans to Velasco, Texas, in 1833. She lived with the Wharton family at Eagle Island until she married Edward Thomas Branch on August 15, 1838, and moved to Liberty County, Texas.

As tensions built between Texans and the Mexican Government, William Wharton became intensely involved with the Texas Revolution. For the better part of four years, Sarah struggled with caring for two young children and maintaining the plantation in his absence. When a group of Texans attacked and overtook the Mexican fort at Velasco, William was one of the signers of the terms of surrender. William was a delegate at the Convention of 1832 and was chosen to present the resolutions approved at the convention to the Mexican government, but they were never allowed to be delivered. William Wharton presided over the proceedings when a new convention was called for in 1833. In late 1835, he went to the siege of San Antonio de Bexar with the Texas Army as a judge advocate but resigned when he was appointed as a commissioner to the United States to secure aid for Texas. Attacks at the Alamo and Goliad, by the advancing Mexican Army, triggered a panic known as the "*Runaway Scrape*," in which the settlers in Texas fled toward the Texas-United States border. Sarah and her two children rushed to the safety of her family at Bernardo Plantation. Beginning March 31, 1836, Sam Houston and the Texas Army camped on the Groce property near Groce's Ferry on the Brazos River. On April 12, 1836, the two iconic cannons called "*The Twin Sisters*" were delivered to the river landing and placed in front of the home at Bernardo. By April 14, with cannons in tow, the Texas Army had crossed the river in route to a clash with the Mexican Army at San Jacinto.

On April 21, 1836, Texas won its independence following an overwhelming victory at the Battle of San Jacinto. Jared Ellison Groce II, patriarch of the Groce family, died at his home in Grimes County, Texas, on November 20, 1836. When Sam Houston became the first elected President of the Republic of Texas, one of his first official acts was to appoint William Wharton, Minister to the United States. Sarah made a brief trip with William to Washington D. C., during which time William was able to persuade President Andrew Jackson to recognize the independence of Texas from Mexico. Some claimed that his success was due in part to Sarah because of her dynamic personality at diplomatic meetings and her active participation at dinners and social events. In 1837, William resigned as minister to run for office in the Texas Senate. He was captured at sea by a Mexican ship and sent to prison in Matamoros. William managed to escape and then made his way home in time to be elected to the Texas Senate in 1838. After six years of turmoil, it appeared that Sarah Wharton's life had become whole again. Her husband William was safe at home, and her adopted daughter Anne was happily married and starting a new life. Her son John Austin was staying at Bernardo and was being taught by a private tutor. At Eagle Island Plantation, William and Sarah often hosted lavish events. After visiting the plantation, Author Mary Austin Holley, a cousin of Stephen F. Austin, noted that the house was filled with *"books and other curiosities."* She described Sarah Wharton as a *"charming woman,"* and *"having a cultivated inquiring mind."*[27]

While the events of 1836 and 1837 certainly tested the resolve of Sarah Wharton, they could not compare with the devastating events of 1838 and 1839. The tragedies began on September 2, 1838, with the death of her namesake, Sarah Wharton Groce, the 3-year-old daughter of older brother Leonard Waller Groce. Sarah's younger brother, Jared Ellison Groce III, died on February 3, 1839. Just six weeks later, on March 14, 1839, her beloved husband William was killed when he accidentally shot himself while stepping down from his horse.

Widowed and grieving from three painful losses, Sarah committed herself to the care and education of her young son, John Austin. In 1846, John was sent to South Carolina College (present-day University of South Carolina), where he became commander of the student cadet corps. While in college, John met Eliza Penelope Johnson, daughter of South Carolina Governor David Johnson. The couple married on February 25, 1851, and soon made their way to Texas, where John began studying law. Two daughters were born to the marriage of John and Penelope Wharton. The first was born in 1852 and was named Sarah Ann in honor of John's mother. The child died at less than one year of age. The second, Kate Ross, was born in 1854.

After becoming licensed to practice law, John partnered with Clinton Terry to form a law firm. Clinton had attended the U. S. Military Academy and was the brother of Benjamin Franklin Terry, who would later command the 8th Texas Cavalry (Terry's Texas Rangers). During the War Between the States, John Wharton helped to organize and was elected Captain of Company B, 8th Texas Cavalry. After Colonel Benjamin F. Terry was killed at Woodson, Kentucky, and Lt. Colonel Thomas S. Lubbock died of illness, John Austin Wharton was promoted to Colonel and commander of the famed unit. At the Battle of Shiloh on April 6, 1862, John was wounded, and his former law partner, Clinton Terry, was killed. Because of his leadership during the battle, John Austin was promoted to Brigadier General. He was promoted in 1864 to the rank of Major General. Near the end of the war, he was back in Texas in charge of all Calvary operations there. While at the headquarters of General John B. Magruder, in the Fannin House Hotel in Houston, Texas, a dispute arose between John and one of his subordinates, Colonel George Wythe Baylor. It was said that John called Baylor a liar and struck him. In anger, Baylor drew his pistol and fired. Major General John Austin Wharton died there on April 6, 1865.[28] He was originally buried at his home at *Eagle Island* but years later was reinterred, with honors, in the Texas State Cemetery.

Sarah Ann Wharton was devastated by the loss of her only child. After John's death, her daughter-in-law Penelope and granddaughter Kate remained at home with her. She loved and nurtured Kate and tended to her education. Tragically, after giving all the love and attention that Sarah could give, her last remaining heir, Kate Ross Wharton, died on August 8, 1872. Her mother, Penelope, died May 15, 1876. Widowed and childless, Sarah Ann Wharton died on February 11, 1878.

Sarah Ann Wharton's contribution to Texas history is a life that was an inspiring model of womanhood. Through good times and bad, she remained dedicated and courageous. Her admiration and respect for her father illustrated the value of preserving heritage and family values. Her compassionate support to her brothers in times of need demonstrated her strength of character. She was a woman who stood beside her husband regardless of the path he chose and contributed to his every effort without abandoning her own ambitions. Her loving dedication to her son and her granddaughter was unparalleled. In short, Sarah Ann Groce Wharton was an extraordinary woman.

Margaret Leatherbury Hallett
(1787 – 1863)

Meeting life's challenges in Mexican Texas took undaunted courage and relentless determination. Margaret Hallet was undoubtedly a woman with those qualifications. She was born to George and Ann Rodgers Leatherby in Stafford County, Virginia, on December 25, 1787. Many of the events in her life before she arrived in Texas are difficult to confirm due to the lack of primary sources. Somewhere between fifteen and eighteen years of age, she fell in love with a merchant seaman named John Hallett. It has been said that her family was unhappy with the romance, but Margaret was determined to be with him and said to her family, "*I would rather marry John Hallett and be the beginning of a new family than remain single and be the tail-end of an old one,*" and left home to be with John in Maryland. They were reportedly married aboard a ship in Chesapeake Bay.[29]

When their first two sons were born, John and Margaret were operating a mercantile business in Matamoros, Mexico. John Jr. was born in 1813, and William Henry in 1815. After their business was confiscated by the Spanish Government, the couple moved to La Bahía (present-day Goliad), Texas. John and Margaret's third son, Benjamin, was born there in 1818, and a daughter, Mary Jane, was born there in 1822. On February 15, 1833, John applied for a grant in Stephen F. Austin's Colony. His application showed that his wife and 2 children were in New York at that time, and 2 sons were with him in La Bahía.[30] Margaret and two of the children returned to La Bahía sometime before the death of her husband in 1836. The date of death of her youngest son Benjamin is unknown, but he was not with Margeret and her daughter Mary Jane when they fled from La Bahía during the "*Runaway Scrape.*" John Hallett, Jr. joined the Texas Army and fought at the Battle of San Jacinto. Records show that he served in Company F, 1st Regiment, Texan Volunteers, under the Command of Colonel Edward Burleson.[31] It has been said that William Hallett went to Matamoros and was captured by the Mexican Army. There is no record of his death. After Texas won its independence at the Battle of San Jacinto, Margaret and her daughter settled on their land in Austin's Colony. John Hallet, Jr., died in 1837. Some say that he was killed by Indians near San Antonio.

37

Widowed with only one remaining child, Margarett planted crops and raised livestock. As more settlers established homes near her property, she opened a store and traded for pelts and hides with members of the Tonkawa Tribe. She sometimes sent hides to nearby Gonzales and traded them for corn.[32] Margaret learned to communicate with the Tonkawa. Legend has it that the local Chief nicknamed her *"brave squaw"* for raising a lump on the head of a brave who was attempting to steal merchandise.[33] In 1838, Margaret donated land near her trading post for a townsite. It was named Hallettsville in her honor.[34] Margaret also built a new home there.

Drawing from portions of Fayette, Colorado, Jackson, Victoria, and Gonzales counties, the Republic of Texas Congress established a judicial county in 1842 named La Baca County. After statehood, it was renamed Lavaca County in 1846. Before selecting a county seat, court sessions were held in the Hallett home. A bitter dispute arose between Hallettsville and the older town of Petersburg over selecting a county seat. Margarett Hallet was an influential person in the county. Margarett's influence likely contributed to the town of Hallettsville being chosen as county seat. Alma Male and Female Institute was founded in 1852 on land donated by Margaret. She helped the board of trustees organize the new school.

The extraordinary life of Margaret Leatherbury Hallett ended in 1863. She was buried at the Hallett League, but in 1952, her remains were reinterred in the Hallettsville City Memorial Park.[35] Sadly, many details of her life are yet undiscovered. What an incredible journey it must have been that took her and John from Chesapeake Bay to Matamoros in New Spain or the turmoil that drove them and their children to La Bahía in Mexican Texas. It is hard to imagine the terror she must have felt from losing her husband and then being forced to flee from a merciless Mexican Army that was destroying everything in its path. It is equally hard to visualize the courage it must have taken to establish a life alone in the wilderness with a young daughter and the grief she must have felt after having lost all three of her sons. Her story ends as one of a courageous and accomplished woman. Possibly the greatest reward for her efforts was given by her only surviving child, Mary Jane. In 1843, Mary Jane Hallett married Collatinus Montague Ballard.[36] During the years prior to Margaret's death, Mary Jane Ballard gave birth to

10 children, and another 2 before the death of her husband in 1867. It was fitting that she would continue the bloodline of a gallant Texan like her mother, Margaret.

Many women during the era of Mexican Texas shared similar stories. Most of those stories were never recorded, and few left such a lasting mark on the history of Texas. Margaret Hallet was one of a kind.

Sarah Jane Newman (Sally Scull)
(1817 – 1876?)

Sarah Newman, Author Unknown, Public Domain

The harsh and sometimes brutal frontier of Mexican Texas sometimes contributed to the development of women who were more ruthless than the environment around them. One such woman was Sarah Jane Newman, more often known as Sally Scull. She is memorialized in history as a gun-carrying cowgirl, horse trader, outlaw, and trail boss who could out cuss, out ride, and out shoot any man alive. She was sometimes referred to as the scariest siren in Texas, including by all of her 5 husbands.

It is believed that Sarah was born around 1817 in Illinois. She came to Texas with her parents, Joseph Austin, and Rachel Elizabeth Newman, in about 1822, along with her grandparents, William and Mary Polly Rabb, as members of Stephen F Austin's Old 300. Joseph Newman received title to a league of land in present-day Wharton County and a labor of land in present-day Austin County on August 10, 1824.[37] Joseph died on February 15, 1831, leaving his widow with Sarah and nine siblings.[38] Sarah's grandparents, William and Mary Rabb, were killed during an Indian attack in 1831 in Fayette County.

While Sarah was still a small child, her family was rescued from an Indian attack by a posse, which included a man named Jesse Robinson. On March 31, 1838, her hero Jesse Robinson became her first husband.[39] The couple had two children, Nancy and Alfred. Although Jesse was a seasoned veteran of the Texas Rangers and the Texas Army, he feared Sarah's propensity to settle arguments at the point of a gun, and he soon got tired of her bad temper. Jesse divorced Sarah in Colorado County, Texas, on March 6, 1843, citing her violent temper and claiming that she was an adulterer and that she had been harboring and feeding a stranger in an old wash house. The divorce

proceeding had been anything other than peaceful. Lending credibility to Jesse's claim about the wash house stranger, records show that on March 20, 1843, Sarah married George H. Scull, in Colorado County.[40]

41

George Scull was a gunsmith by trade and served in the Texas Army as a volunteer law enforcement officer. Although Sarah had re-married, it is apparent that the bitter dispute between her and her ex-husband, Jesse, was not over. About nineteen months after her new marriage, Sarah sold her livestock, farm equipment, 400 acres of her inheritance, and George's gunsmith tools. On December 30, 1844, she petitioned for custody of her daughter. When custody was denied, Sarah and George abducted both children and headed toward New Orleans, Louisiana, and placed the children in a convent where they would be safe and get an education. Jesse tracked them down but, rather than taking them back to Texas, placed them in yet another convent. A tug-of-war ensued over the children and continued for years.

By 1849, Sarah was reportedly single. George had vanished from her life without a trace for some unknown reason. Sarah claimed that he died, while others speculated that he may have run out in the middle of the night to escape her wrath. Either way, George would not be Sarah's only husband, who mysteriously disappeared. Apparently, Sarah liked the name *"Scull."* For much of the rest of her life, she would refer to herself as *"Sally Scull"* or *"Sally Skull."* Folklore says that some parents in early Texas would promote good conduct from the children by telling them, *"If you don't behave, Sally Skull will get you."*

In 1852, Sarah moved to Nueces County, Texas, where she bought a 150-acre ranch near the town of Banquete. In the memoirs of legendary Texas Ranger John Salmon *"Rip"* Ford, he tells a story about an encounter with Sarah, writing:

> *"The last incident attracting the writer's attention occurred while he was at Kinney's Tank, winding his way homewards from Corpus Christi Fair, 1852. He heard the report of a pistol, raised his eyes, saw a man falling to the ground and a woman not far from him in the act of lowering a six-shooter. She was a noted character named Sally Scull. She was famed as a rough fighter, and prudent men did not willingly provoke her into a row. It was understood that she was justifiable in what she did on this occasion, having acted in self-defense."*

So many similar accounts of Sarah's hot temper suggest that rather than self-defense, it is more likely a case of Sarah deciding that the man just needed to die. On October 17, 1852,[41] John Boyle became her 3rd husband. He was instrumental in helping Sarah to build a thriving cattle business. Just like husband #2, John Boyle mysteriously vanished. The number of stories that explain his disappearance was countless and only added to the legend of Sally Skull. One such story tells of a time when, out of fear, John attempted to ambush her, but she beat him to the punch. Yet another tells that John and Sarah went on a drinking binge and spent the night at a hotel in Corpus Christi, after which John attempted to wake her the next morning by dumping water on her face, and Sarah awoke with a pistol from under her pillow and shot him to death. One of my favorites tells that Sarah caught her drunken husband drinking from a whiskey barrel, pushed him headfirst into the barrel, and sealed it up. A less dramatic story tells that John drowned while attempting to drive an ox-driven wagon across a swollen river. All of these are the things that make legends. It reminds me of an old Texas saying: *"Don't let the truth get in the way of a good story."*

The story of Sarah's 4th marriage is a little hard to believe. According to the story, Sarah married Isaiah Watkins on December 20, 1855. She was only for five months. Her court filings in her divorce case reportedly stated that he beat her and dragged her for almost 200 yards. Knowing the character and reputation of "Sally Skull," it is hard to believe that she did not shoot him to death rather than divorce him. It is also said that Sally proved Watkins was living with a woman named Juanita. Her divorce was supposedly granted on the grounds of cruelty and adultery. This marriage may also have been more legend than fact.

By 1860, Sally Skull was at the height of her notoriety. She was known at every corner of Texas and miles beyond. But now, she was about to take her 5th husband, and this one would be her undoing. In December of 1860, Sarah married William Horsdorff, a man half her age. The onset of the War Between the States brought new financial opportunities for Sarah. Cotton was still king, and the merchants of Europe were hungry for it. The Union Navy had blockaded the Southern ports, but international law prevented the United States from interfering with Mexican maritime trade. The trail to Matamoros became the "Cotton Road" and the lifeline of the Confederacy. Sarah was in a perfect position to haul cotton to Mexico, which could be traded for weapons and ammunition for the Confederacy. Sarah spoke fluent Spanish and had little trouble exchanging Cotton at the Mexican border. She prospered well during the war years. Her husband, Horsdorff, was given the nickname *"Horse Trough"* by some of her associates. One day after the War, she rode off with her husband, but only *"Horse Trough"* returned. Upon his arrival, he said, *"She simply disappeared,"* and gave no other explanation. The infamous *"Sally Skull"* was no more. A short time later, a drifter reported running across a woman's body in a shallow grave on the prairie, but there was no evidence that it was the body of Sarah. Despite random reports of her being sighted in South Texas, none of the reports were ever confirmed.

Despite her many shortcomings, Sarah was said to be a loving mother and many noted that she never betrayed a friend. She competed and succeeded as a woman living in a man's world and survived in a brutal and dangerous atmosphere without fear. An attribute that was clearly Texan.

Chapter 3 – The Republic of Texas
(1836 – 1845)

The steady stream of Anglo-American immigrants into Texas in the early nineteenth century changed the culture and social structure of Mexican Texas forever. By 1835, the Anglo population had grown to more than 20,000. More than 5 to 1 compared to the approximate 4,000 Hispanic citizens. For the most part, the Anglo settlers were content and loyal to the Mexican government, due primarily to the autonomy and privileges given to them by the Mexican Constitution adopted in 1824.

The attitude of both Hispanic and Anglo citizens began to change when Antonio López de Santa Anna was elected President of Mexico in 1833. By 1834, the Republic of Mexico's government was no longer a democracy and had transformed into an autocratic state. In 1835, Santa Anna created a new centralist government and replaced the Constitution of 1824 with the *"Siete Leyes (seven laws)."* As tensions grew, a brief skirmish occurred when new Mexican troops appeared at Anahuac to collect customs duties, but the disturbance ended quickly. The spark that caused the fire of revolution occurred near the town of Gonzales after Mexican authorities demanded the return of a cannon that had been given to settlers for protection years prior. When the citizens refused to return the cannon, a Mexican force of 100 dragoons was sent from San Antonio to retrieve it. On October 2, 1835, the dragoons were attacked by a superior number of Texian Militiamen, forcing the Mexican soldiers to retreat. Although it was a short conflict, the resolve of the Texians was clearly demonstrated. The war for Texas Independence was underway, and there was no turning back.

Knowing that the Mexican government was sure to retaliate, the Texians quickly began recruiting an army. By the end of 1835, the Texian Army had captured forts at Goliad (La Bahía) and San Antonio de Béxar. Determined to quell the uprising, Santa Anna's army crossed the Rio Grande River on February 16, 1836, and arrived at Béxar on February 23. After 13 days of fighting, the Mexican forces defeated the Texian Army at the Alamo, killing every defender inside. On March 20, 1836, a Texian force under the command of James Fannin surrendered to Mexican General José de Urrea, and more than 300 men were executed. Santa Anna's army continued forward in pursuit of Sam Houston's Texas Army, destroying everything in its wake. Settlers fled aside the Texas Army toward Nacogdoches to escape. After crossing the Brazos River near Groce's Ferry, the Texas Army changed courses and turned east toward Harrisburg. At the confluence of the Buffalo Bayou and the San Jacinto River, The Texian forces routed the Mexican Army, captured Santa Anna, and guaranteed independence for Texas.

While now a free and independent nation, Texas still had more than its share of problems. It was still a wild frontier, and suddenly, it had to deal with raising money, establishing trade with the United States and other countries, and defending its borders. As the first President of the Republic of Texas, Sam Houston served from October 22, 1836, to December 10, 1838. He spent a great deal of time trying to establish peaceful relations between the various Indian tribes and white settlers.

Life for women in the Republic of Texas was little changed from the days of Mexican rule. Texas was still a wilderness, filled with danger. Not only did a woman have to be skilled with a frying pan and rub-board, but she had to know her way around a gun and a knife. Life in Texas was hard regardless of race or gender. Although women still lived in a society dominated primarily by men, their role was crucial in sustaining survival on the frontier. In many ways, women in the Republic of Texas had more rights than women in most of the United States. A limited degree of Castilian Law had carried over from Spanish Texas to the new republic. Single women or widows were allowed to own property, file suit in court, make contracts, or make their own will. A married woman could be declared *"feme sole,"* meaning that her rights were not legally subordinated by her husband, and she could retain her property and manage her affairs as if she were a single woman. However, a married woman's rights were only as great as her ability to enforce them.

It took a special kind of woman to venture into the unknown wilderness, and staying there could be even more challenging. Even the strongest women often faced dangers such as disease, complications from childbirth, exposure to the elements, Indian raids, snake bites, and animal attacks. In a lawless frontier, these women were often at the mercy of ruthless men eager to exploit their vulnerability. Yet, it is these powerful stories of courage and resilience that weave the rich tapestry of Texas history.

Susanna Wilkerson Dickinson
(1814 – 1883)

Susanna Dickinson, Courtesy of DRT Library; Public Domain

A classic example of the strength and determination of the women of early Texas is the story of Susanna Dickinson. Despite suffering two decades of grief, heartbreak, and abuse, Susanna never lost her love for the land that was once the object of a dream shared by her and her first husband, Almeron. She is often remembered as a survivor of the Battle of the Alamo. Still, her story is much bigger than that, and her ability to rise above adversity is truly an inspiration to all Texans.

Susanna Arabella Wilkerson was born about 1814 in Tennessee. There is very little information about her family or the date and exact location of her birth. She married Almaron Dickinson in Bolivar, Tennessee, on May 24, 1829. Almaron, a blacksmith by trade, was born about 1800 in Pennsylvania and was nearly twice Susanna's age. He had previously served as an artilleryman in the United States Army. Soon after the marriage, the dream of owning thousands of acres of land lured the couple to the Mexican Province of Texas. The couple arrived in the DeWitt Colony in 1831, where Almaron received a league of land (4,428 acres) on the east bank of the San Marcos River below the Old Bexar Road in present-day Caldwell County.[42] He later acquired property in Gonzales, where he opened a blacksmith shop and partnered with George C. Kimbell in a hat-making business.[43] The couple's first and only child, Angeline Elizabeth Dickinson, was born on December 14, 1834. Soon, their dreams and lives would be changed forever.

In September of 1835, the Mexican Government demanded residents of Gonzales to return a cannon that had been given them years earlier for defense of the colonists against Indian attacks. The colonists angrily replied: "Come and take it!" When a Mexican force of 100 men, led by Lt. Francisco de Castañeda, reached the Guadalupe River near Gonzales, he was met on the opposite bank by 18 armed Texians. Among those renowned "*Old Eighteen*" was Almaron Dickinson.[44] Castañeda camped on the west side of the river. On the night of October 1, 1835, more than 140 Texians crossed the river and attacked the Mexican forces. Being outnumbered, Castañeda retreated, and the Texas Revolution had begun. Hostilities and the Texian Army continued to grow. On October 13, 1835, Susanna said goodbye to her husband as he left with the Texas Army, laying siege to the town of Bexar (San Antonio). After the Texas Army took control of Bexar in early December, Susanna and her infant daughter re-joined Almaron and stayed at the home of Ramón Músquiz.

By February 23, 1836, many residents of Bexar began to evacuate in advance of the imminent arrival of the Mexican Army under General Santa Anna. Susanna, with her daughter Angelina, took shelter in the Alamo Chapel. By nightfall, Mexican soldiers began positioning themselves around the Alamo, and the siege had begun. On February 25, a cold front dropped the temperature into the 30s. Neither Army was prepared for the cold. On the morning of March 1, 1836, under the cover of darkness, Lieutenant George C. Kimbell entered the Alamo with his force of 32 men from Gonzales to reinforce the fort. The small force of Texas volunteers continued the fight against impossible odds, but around 6:30 AM on March 6, 1836, the Mexican Army launched its final assault, killing every soldier in the compound. The battle lasted less than 90 minutes. One account related that near the end of the final attack, Almaron went to his wife and said: *"Great God, Sue! The Mexicans are inside our walls! All is lost! If they spare you, save my child."* *"Then, with a parting kiss, he drew his sword and plunged into the strife, then raging in different portions of the fortifications."*[45] It is important to understand that there are discrepancies in all accounts of the siege of the Alamo. Even in the accounts given by Susanna, you must note that she could not read and write and was trying to relay events that occurred during a traumatic tragedy. Her collection of accounts came from many interviews over the course of many years.

After the battle, whether accidentally or deliberately, Susanna was struck by a bullet and required treatment. She was later taken back to the Músquiz home, where she was interviewed by Santa Anna. It was said that he offered to adopt Angelina and take her to Mexico City, where she could be cared for and educated. Susanna refused the offer. She and Angelina were escorted toward Gonzales by a former slave named Ben. She was given a blanket, a horse, 2 silver pesos, and a message for the leader of the Texas Army. They were joined along the way by Joe, the slave of William Travis, who had also survived the battle. General Houston had dispatched Erastus *"Deaf"* Smith from Gonzales to retrieve news about the Alamo. He discovered Susanna and his escorts near Cibolo Crossing just northwest of Bexar. From there, they continued toward Gonzales over rugged terrain. It seems incredible that Susanna was able to continue the journey. She was heartbroken, wounded, and cold. Having lost everything but her daughter and the clothes on her back, Susanna valiantly completed the trip to Gonzales and, on March 12, personally delivered the message from Santa Anna to Sam Houston.

Once General Sam Houston was informed of the fall of the Alamo and received the warning from Mexican General Santa Anna, he decided upon an immediate retreat to the Colorado River and ordered all inhabitants of Gonzales to accompany him. This began the mass exodus known as the *"Runaway Scrape."* He ordered the town of Gonzales to be burned to deny Santa Anna's advancing army food, shelter, and supplies. Not everyone was happy about having to destroy their personal property, but Houston was determined to slow the advance of the Mexican Army. Having no money and no protection for herself and her daughter, Susanna had to follow the others, fleeing Gonzales.

After a series of retreats, the Texas Army camped near the Brazos River at Bernardo Plantation, the first and largest cotton plantation in Texas and the home of Jared E. Groce. There, the Army trained and drilled for two weeks. It would be interesting to know if Susanna was present to witness the grandeur of Bernardo during a time when she was at the very depth of poverty.

While camped at Bernardo, the Texas Army received two cannons that were gifts from the City of Cincinnati. With their new cannons in tow, the Texas Army crossed the swollen Brazos River on the steamboat *"Yellow Stone."* The Army reached Spring Creek on April 16, and the next day, to the delight of his men, Sam Houston made the dramatic decision to turn toward Harrisburg to engage the waiting Mexican Army. The Texas Revolution drew to an end when, at the confluence of the Buffalo Bayou and the San Jacinto River, the Texas Army defeated the Mexican Army at the Battle of San Jacinto. The short 18-minute battle resulted in the capture of President/General Santa Anna and an end to his tyranny. The Republic of Texas was born.

Susanna's name was not recorded again until October 1836, when she petitioned the newly formed Texas Government for a $500 pension. Her pension was denied. It is almost inconceivable that a woman who paid so dearly to become a Texan and remained so dedicated to a land that she and her former husband loved could be abandoned by its own government. Her situation had gone from bad to desperate. She was, at the time, a twenty-two-year-old widow, still grieving from the horrifying death of her husband. She had a two-year-old daughter, no money, and few prospects. The next twenty years of her life would bring even more desperation. There are references to actions and events during those two decades that might suggest flaws in her character, but they cannot overshadow the examples of her strength and courage. Sometimes, desperate people do desperate things.

In need of some financial assistance and a male protector, Susanna was cohabitating with a man approximately her age by June 1837. Little is known about him other than his name was John Williams. The couple was married in Harrisburg County (Now Harris County) on November 27, 1837. From the beginning of the marriage, John was abusive to Susanna and her 3-year-old daughter Angelina. Susanna filed for divorce, claiming that Williams had failed to provide support for her and her daughter, exercising force enough to cause her to miscarry a child and beating and abusing her daughter. The divorce granted on March 24, 1838, was one of the first divorces granted in the County.

At the age of 24, Susanna married Francis Parham Herring in Harrisburg County, on December 20, 1838.[46] Herring was born in Georgia in 1816 and was 2 years younger than Susanna. There were unconfirmed accounts that Susanna was working for Pamelia Mann at the infamous Mansion House Hotel at the time of her marriage to Herring. They also claimed that Susanna opened a boarding house in Houston after the State Capital was moved to Austin. Francis Herring died in 1843. His obituary stated that he died from digestive fever, but reportedly, the actual cause of his death was alcoholism. Susanna apparently never disclosed to any of her husbands that the heirs of Almaron Dickinson were awarded 640 acres of land in Clay County, Texas, in about 1839 for his service in the Texas Army and another 1,920 acres at a later date.

On December 7, 1847, Susanna married Peter Belles (also known as Bellis or Bellows) in Harris County. Belles was born in Pennsylvania around 1810. The 1850 U. S. Census showed Susanna and Angelina in the household of Peter Belles in Houston's First Ward. A 20-year-old German-born woman listed as R. E. Goodbaker was also shown in the household.[47] It was said that Belles was a poor provider, and that Susanna had to support the family by running a boarding house. In 1849, Susanna's life began to change when she attended the First Baptist Church of Houston where Dr. Rufus C. Burleson was pastor. Burleson described his first meeting with Susanna, saying,

> *"Wednesday night at prayer meeting I saw five or six persons weeping under deep conviction, and then, according to my custom, I invited all who wanted to be saved to come forward for special prayer. Among those who came forward with tears and penitential sobs, was Mrs. Dickenson, who had become Mrs. Bells. She was nominally a member of the Episcopal Church, But with many tears she said she never knew anything about her lost condition or the true mission of the church, till she heard that sermon on Sunday night. I visited her at her home, and wept and prayed with her. I found her a great bundle of untamed passions, devoted in her love and bitter in her hate. After many tears and prayers and religious instruction, she was joyfully converted. In less than two months her change was so complete as to be observed by all her neighbors. At least 1,500 people crowded the Banks of Buffalo Bayou on Sabbath evening to see her baptized."*

Susanna and Burleson forged a life-long friendship. In 1851, a young man named John Maynard Griffith stayed at the boarding house. Susanna found him to be an upstanding Christian from a good family, in the County of Montgomery. Desperately wanting to remove her daughter from the horrible environment in which she had been raised, Susanna vigorously promoted Angelina to pursue the young man and soon arranged a marriage between the two. Rufus Burleson was asked to officiate at the wedding, and he later reflected in his memoirs,

> *"The babe of the Alamo, whose infant eyes looked upon the horrors of the Alamo, grew up to womanhood full of life, and fun and frolic.*

Under the well-meant, pious persuasions of her mother, she married a good, honest, hardworking Baptist man from the country. When I performed the marriage ceremony, I shuddered to see two such uncongenial spirits united in marriage. Marriages for money, for position, for convenience, or from parental persuasion, are often fearful mistakes. Marriage should never be from anything but real love, springing from the heart, guided by the head and limited by conscience. When people marry where they do not love, they are apt to love where they have not married."

After the marriage, Angelina moved with John to the Griffith family property in Montgomery County, near the town of Dobbin. Over the following 6 years, she gave birth to a daughter and two sons.

In 1855, the year of Angelina's 21st birthday, Susanna escaped from the desperate life that had plagued her for almost 20 years. With no apparent warning to her husband, Susanna sold the league of land where she and Almaron began their lives together in Texas and moved back to Caldwell County, where she bought a small parcel of land in the town of Lockhart.[48] In 1857, her husband Peter Belles filed a vengeful divorce petition claiming that Susanna had abandoned him and was guilty of having lived in a house of ill fame and further claimed that she was in constant habit of committing adultery with various persons.

It is uncertain whether any of the claims were true. Susanna made no attempt to answer the suit or show up in court. By then, she had met a skilled and industrious man named Joseph William Hannig. He was an immigrant from Germany and operated a cabinet shop in Lockhart. Most records show that he was born in 1834. He was almost twenty years younger than Susanna. The couple was married on December 9, 1857. [49]

It is likely that Susanna and Angelina sold the 2,560 acres in Clay County prior to 1860, which could have been a contributing factor to Angelina's journey down a road to ruin. After Angelina's third child, Joseph William Hannig Griffith, was born in 1857, she began drinking and partying. Her marriage was clearly headed toward divorce. Rufus Burleson noted in his memoirs:

"Soon the vivacious city girl got tired of her country home and her amiable, plodding husband. Alienations, repinings and divorce followed. The mother's heart bled over the ruin of her child's happiness. The unhappy daughter drifted off to New Orleans. The mother, with her undying love, followed the daughter."

At some time before 1862, Angelina abandoned her husband and three children and eventually made her way to New Orleans. It has been said that John went searching for her but never found her. Their two youngest children were sent to live with their grandmother Susanna in Austin, and the oldest son was left with one of John's brothers. Much of the rest of Angelina's life is a mystery, but at one point, she was married to a man named Oscar Holmes and gave birth to her fourth child, Sarah Ann Holmes on September 6, 1865, but as before, Angelina abandoned her husband and child to live the wild life. Sarah was retrieved from a convent in Louisiana by her grandmother Susanna and taken to live with her and two of her siblings in Austin. Angelina's death is also a mystery. It was reported that Susanna received a message that said Angelina died of a "uterus rupture" in New Orleans in 1870, but a news article claimed that she died from the same cause in Galveston in 1869. The article went on to state that she lived the life of a courtesan. How the tragic story truly ended will likely never be known.

Susanna loved her daughter and her grandchildren unconditionally. Just as she tried so desperately to protect and provide for the daughter she loved so deeply, she was equally as loving toward her grandchildren and stayed so until her death. Her last years were happy and prosperous. She died in Austin, Texas on October 7, 1883, and was buried in Oakwood Cemetery. After Susanna's death, her husband, Joseph William Hannig married Louise Staacke, and lived in San Antonio for the rest of his life. Although he had remarried, he was buried beside Susanna in Oakwood Cemetery.

The passing of Susanna Dickinson Hannig occurred less than six months after the State of Texas purchased the Alamo from the Catholic Church, the place that had ended the dreams of a loving couple and yet defined their roles in Texas history. She became the voice of the Alamo narrative. With strength and determination, she overcame her loss during that harrowing struggle and yet again with the tragic passing of her only child. Amidst her grief, she gained renewed faith to guide her through her darkest times. Her saga concluded as a shining example of courage and resiliency. A fitting end to her story is found in the memoirs of her friend Dr. Rufus C. Burleson, where he wrote:

> *"I am rejoiced to know she died happy in Jesus and respected and beloved by all who knew her. Thus, lived and died the Heroine of the Alamo, whose tragic history and wonderful conversion are so full of marvelous events and so rich in material for reflection."* [50]

Pamelia Dickinson Mann
(unknown – 1840)

Another example of a strong woman created by a harsh environment is Pamelia Dickinson Mann. She reached the height of her notoriety and fortune in the formative days of Houston, Texas. The town was founded on the muddy banks of Buffalo Bayou. In those early days, Houston was infamous for five things: drunkenness, dueling, brawling, prostitution, and profanity, and on any given day, Pamelia might have been right in the middle of it. There are no portraits of Pamelia, but she was described as a full-bodied woman with enough charm to attract most men. She also possessed a bold attitude and was skilled with a knife and a gun.

Pamelia was likely born shortly before 1800. Her first husband was only identified by the last name Hunt, by which she had one son, Flournoy Nimrod Hunt, born around 1817. Pamelia's second husband was Samuel William Allen, by which she had another son, Samuel Ezekiel William Allen, born in Frankfort, Kentucky, on January 2, 1826. On May 2, 1830, Pamelia married Marshall Mann.[51] The couple arrived in Texas in about 1834 and settled near San Felipe, Texas. While perfectly capable of handling frontier life, she never favored a life of farming or ranching. In March 1836, Pamelia was operating a boarding house in the community of Washington, more than 50 miles upriver from San Felipe.[52] There, she fed and boarded delegates and concerned citizens attending the Constitutional Convention as Texas declared its independence from Mexico. After the convention, she returned to San Felipe. Pamelia and her family were forced to evacuate San Felipe during the "*Runaway Scrape*" in 1836. During her flight from the advancing Mexican Army, Pamelia met Texas Army General Sam Houston. She also met and befriended Susanna Dickinson, who, along with infant daughter Angelina, survived the massacre at the Alamo.

It was when the Texas Army camped at Groce's Crossing on the Brazos River that Pamelia's most famous escapade took place. Although there are several versions of the story, it was said that General Sam Houston negotiated a deal with Pamelia to borrow a team of oxen from her. After spending some time in the General's tent and sharing some corn liquor, Pamelia agreed to loan him the oxen so long as they were traveling the same path as she was toward the Trinity River. Some distance after crossing the Brazos River, Sam Houston made his fateful decision to turn eastward toward Harrisburg to encounter the Mexican Army. Upon discovering that the Army was changing course, Pamelia rode up to Sam Houston, screaming, swearing, and threatening to draw arms. She told General Houston that no matter which direction the Texas Army went, the oxen were going with her toward the Trinity River. Houston attempted to plead his case but to no avail. Pamelia dismounted, unhitched the team, remounted, and rode away with the oxen. It is uncertain how far Pamelia got on her journey. It has been said that Susanna Dickinson and her infant daughter Angelina accompanied her. Shortly after the Battle of San Jacinto, Pamelia's husband, Marshall, joined the Texas Army and served through at least September 1836.

By August 1836, Pamelia and her two sons were in Harrisburg; by March 1837, they were in Houston, and in June 1837, Pamelia was operating a hotel that she named the Mansion House. It was located at the corner of Congress and Milam Streets. Details of how Pamelia became the owner of the hotel are confusing. One account says that she bought two city lots at that location on March 3, 1837, but it seems unlikely that a structure of that type could be built and furnished in 90 days. Another account says that she purchased the hotel from Benjamin Fort Smith on June 8, 1837. Regardless of its origin, the Mansion House was a fine establishment, just blocks from the Texas Capitol. It was described as a two-story, plastered building with porches. The upper store contained private rooms with washstands, mirrors, and double beds for the hotel's more elite guests and dormitory-style rooms for guests with more limited means. The parlor and dining areas were on the first floor. Guests at the hotel included government leaders, congressmen, military leaders, the very wealthy, and the everyday traveler. The hotel was frequented by President Sam Houston, President Mirabeau B. Lamar, and Dr. Ashbel Smith.

Pamelia's husband, Marshall Mann, died on October 4, 1838, and was buried on his property near San Felipe.[53] Shortly after his death, Pamelia took up with a young man named Tandy K. Brown. On May 8, 1839, a Harris County Grand Jury indicted the couple for fornication, but it never came to trial. On August 2, 1839, Pamelia and Tandy signed a marriage contract stating that all of her property would be retained as if she were a single woman, and they were married 2 days later.

Throughout her years in Texas, Pamelia had been charged with numerous crimes but was only convicted of one. On December 7, 1838, a grand jury indicted her for *"dealing in forgery,"* a crime that in the Republic of Texas was punishable by death.[54] Despite the best efforts of her attorneys, Sam Houston and John Birdsall, Pamelia was found guilty and sentenced to hang. Before the sentence could be carried out, she received a full pardon from President Mirabeau B. Lamar.

On September 7, 1840, Tandy K. Brown died in Houston, Texas, as a result of yellow fever.[55] He was no older than twenty-eight at the time. Pamelia was probably already suffering from the same disease when she died on November 4, 1840. She was buried in an unmarked grave in what is now Founder's Park Cemetery.[56] She left an estate appraised at more than $40,000.

Pamelia Dickinson Hunt Allen Mann Brown was far from a saintly figure. She was disliked by some, yet loved and respected by others. Throughout her adventures in Texas, Pamelia impacted the lives of many. With her rugged yet charming demeanor, she left a lasting and distinctive impression on the culture, heritage and history of Texas.

Margaret Robertson Wright
(1789 – 1879)

Few women were more dedicated to establishing the Republic of Texas than Margaret Theresa Robertson Wright. Her patriotic contributions to the Texas Revolution were a testimony to her strong and courageous character. Though living in a man's world on the frontier of Texas, she remained independent and resilient throughout her years in the Lone Star State.

Margaret was probably born in New Orleans, Louisiana, in about 1789, supposedly to a French mother and an English Father. One record suggests that she was born in New York, and yet another suggests she was born in Pennsylvania. Around 1805, She married a South Carolina man named James Williams Hays. The couple settled near Opelousas, Louisiana, where they had two daughters and a son. Sometime after 1811, the family moved to Bayou Pierre. James died shortly after that and was possibly a casualty of the War of 1812.

After the death of James Hayes, Margaret became the common-law wife of Felix Trudeau, former Commandant of Fort St. Jean Baptiste in Natchitoches, Louisiana.[57] Trudeau was Commandant on April 26, 1804, when at 11.00 a.m., the Spanish flag was lowered and the French flag raised, and at noon, the French flag was lowered and the American flag raised. Margaret and Felix had a daughter born about 1816 and a second daughter born about 1821. Felix Trudeau died in Natchitoches, Louisiana, on February 9, 1822.

Margaret arrived in DeWitt's Colony in about 1825, using the name Madame Trudeau. About a year later, she moved to De León's Colony at Guadalupe Victoria. There, she applied for a league of land on the west bank of the Guadalupe River. She was mentioned in letters between Stephen F. Austin and James Kerr, in 1826 through 1827.[58] In the letters, Kerr says that Margaret was witness to threats made by Martín De León against Green DeWitt and his colonists. In 1828, Margaret married John David Wright, and shortly after they married, Margaret received title to her league of land, and Wright settled on the land with her. The couple had two daughters. Emma Ann Wright was born about 1830, and Tennessee Ann Wright was born May 12, 1834. Early on, John and Margaret's marriage was troubled, leading to

61

long periods of Separation. By about 1835, John had secretly gained title to Margaret's land. The following year, he ran off to the Rio Grande Valley to avoid prosecution for an old debt back in Mississippi. He hid there under the protection of the Mexican government for seven years.[59]

In her husband's absence, Margaret continued to raise cattle on her property. During the Texas Revolution in 1836, approximately 400 Texas soldiers, under the command of Colonel James Fannin, were stationed at the presidio in Goliad. On March 20, 1836, at the Battle of Coleto, Fannin and his men surrendered to Mexican General José de Urrea and were marched back to Goliad. On March 27, 1836, more than 300 Texas soldiers, including Colonel Fannin, were marched out and executed. About 28 of the men, while seriously wounded, managed to escape. One of these escapees, William L. Hunter, managed to make it to Margaret Wright's ranch house on the Guadalupe River. Margaret kept him hidden from Mexican soldiers and nursed him to health. In the process, she learned of other escapees. Risking her life and the loss of her property, Margaret managed to furnish aid and supplies to some of the other men. She set up a system whereby men could leave notes in a hollow tree. She would then retrieve the notes and smuggle medicine and food to them by pretending to draw water from the river. In one case, Margaret managed to steal a gun from Mexican soldiers camped on her property and give it to one of the men still hiding there. She continued to aid the men until they were well and able enough to rejoin the Texas Army. Margaret was never forgotten for bravely saving the men, and more than twenty years later, during a campaign speech at Victoria, Sam Houston praised her for her heroism and called her the "Mother of Texas."[60]

In 1842, John Wright returned from Rio Grande Valley. He soon learned that Margaret had purchased an additional half-league of land while he was gone and deeded 640 acres of it to her son, Peter Hays. John Wright immediately filed a suit against her, claiming that control of their joint property was vested in him and could not be conveyed without his consent. At trial, the court ruled that because she had been an abandoned wife, she was *feme sole* at the time that the transactions took place. John Wright also lost the preliminary appeal. In 1847, Margaret's son, Peter Hays, was killed in an ambush in the Rio Grande Valley. Convinced that John Wright was somehow involved, Margaret filed for divorce on March 6, 1848. In the petition, she claimed that Wright was guilty of habitual cruelty, fraudulent land title transfer, and the murder of Peter Hays. After 3 appeals in the Texas Supreme Court, Margaret was granted a divorce. In the settlement, she received 5,535 acres of land and 570 heads of cattle. In 1850, Margaret sold her interest in the property and moved to Victoria, Texas.[61]

The historical marker, placed by the city on Memorial Drive in Victoria, states that Margaret Theresa Robertson Wright died October 21, 1878.[62] The year of death given on her grave marker in Evergreen Cemetery shows 1879. The simple stone marker is also engraved with a message about how, at the risk of her own life, she cared for the wounded who escaped from the Goliad Massacre.

Margaret Robertson Wright lived for 90 years, with 65 of those years spent in Texas. Most of this time was spent without the support or protection of a husband. While records do not specify how many of those years were dedicated to raising children, she gave birth to seven. She arrived in Texas as a 36-year-old widow and successfully claimed and maintained her own land, all while protecting herself and her children from the many dangers of frontier life. Additionally, she offered aid to those in need. Margaret's story embodies the spirit of courage and compassion that defines Texas, leaving an enduring legacy of bravery and resilience.

Rosalie von Roeder Kleberg
(1813 - 1907)

Rosalie von Reader Kleberg
Creator unknown
Courtesy of Hathi Trust Digital Library
Image is in the Public Domain

Born to an affluent family in Germany, Rosalie von Roeder Kleberg journeyed from a refined world of aristocracy to a rugged frontier that she would soon call home. After leaving behind the comforts of her European upbringing, she arrived in the Mexican state of Texas just as a violent revolution was beginning to unfold. With remarkable courage, she adapted to life as a pioneer and eventually integrated with the family that owned the massive Santa Gertrudis Ranch.

Philippine Sophie Caroline Luise Rosalie von Roeder was born in the Province of Westphalia, Kingdom of Prussia, to Ludwig Siegismund Anton and Caroline Luise von Roeder on July 20, 1813. Her father was a Lieutenant in the Royal Prussian Army.

On March 9, 1831, a man named Johann Friedrich Ernst arrived with his family in Harrisburg, Texas. They were the first German family to immigrate to Mexican Texas. Ernst was granted a league of land in the Stephen F. Austin Colony, close to present-day Industry, Texas. In February 1832, he wrote a letter to a friend in Germany, describing the beauty of Texas and the opportunities it offered. This letter was widely distributed in German communities and attracted the attention of many German citizens, including members of the von Roeder family. By 1834, the von Roeder family had decided to immigrate to Texas.

As the family discussed plans for the move, they decided to send the unmarried members first, including sons Louis, Albrecht, Joachim, their sister Valesca, and a servant named Pollhart. Once they knew that their family members had arrived safely in Texas, the rest of the family planned to do the same. Meanwhile, another Lieutenant in the Royal Prussian Army and a friend of the family, Robert Justus Kleberg, proposed to Rosalie. She agreed to marry him, but only if he immigrated to Texas. Kleberg accepted her terms, and the couple was married on September 4, 1834. The newlyweds and the rest of the von Roeder family set sail for America on September 30. After

sailing for sixty days on the sloop named the *"Congress,"* they arrived in New Orleans. After staying there for two weeks, they boarded a schooner named the *"Sabine"* bound for Brazoria, Texas.[63]

On December 22, 1834, the *"Sabine"* wrecked 50 yards off the shore of Galveston Island. Robert Kleberg described Galveston Island as "a perfect wilderness inhabited only by deer, wolves, and rattlesnakes." Three days after the shipwreck, a steamer called the *"Ocean"* anchored near the camp and sent a small boat ashore. The captain informed them he could only take a few passengers, so Robert Kleberg and Rudolph von Roeder boarded the ship, bound for Brazoria, hoping to find their other family members. Unable to find a boat to take them up the river, Robert and Rudolph decided to travel on foot to San Felipe. There, they met Colonel Frank Johnson and Captain Mosley Baker, who provided information about the family member's whereabouts. They explained that Joachim and Valesca had already died, but Louis, Albrecht, and their servant were in a hut about 14 miles away. When Louis and Albrecht were healthy enough to travel, Robert chartered a small vessel to take them back to Galveston.[64]

Upon their arrival in Galveston, the Kleberg family found their fellow travelers in good spirits, a welcome respite after their arduous journey from Germany. The following day, Robert Kleberg transported Rosalie (Rosa) and her family by boat to Harrisburg. There, he secured a rental house, providing a much-needed sense of stability after the prolonged and challenging transatlantic voyage. With this, the initial phase of their immigration was complete, and Robert and Rosa could finally begin establishing their new life in Texas. While the ensuing winter of 1835 proved harsh, the arrival of spring and summer brought renewed hope and a sense of optimism. Robert and Rosa's brothers, recognizing the immediate need for suitable housing, then departed Harrisburg with essential supplies, traveling to their land grant in Cat Spring, Austin County. Their purpose was to clear land and construct dwellings in preparation for their families. By the fall of 1835, they had successfully erected two log homes sufficient to accommodate their families. The families then relocated from Harrisburg to Cat Spring, bringing only the most basic necessities and leaving the remainder of their belongings behind. At their new settlement in the wilderness, Rosa gave birth to a daughter, Clara Sigismunde Kleberg, on November 29, 1835, marking a huge milestone in their new life in Texas.[65]

The conflict between Texan settlers and Mexican forces in Gonzales created a tense atmosphere. Rosa's brothers, Louis and Albrecht, enlisted in the Texas Army and participated in the Siege of Béxar in December 1835. After the fall of the Alamo, Rosa and her family evacuated their home in Cat Spring and joined other settlers during what became known as the "*Runaway Scrape.*" The advancing Mexican Army captured the town of Harrisburg and destroyed everything in it, including many of Rosa and her family's possessions that had been left in storage. Robert Kleberg and Rosa's brother Louis von Roeder served in the Texas Army under Captain Mosely Baker and fought at the Battle of San Jacinto.[66]

By November 1836, the Kleberg family had returned to their home in Cat Spring, where they would remain for over a decade. During these years, Rosa gave birth to four more children. Their daughter, Johanna Caroline Kleberg, was born on November 29, 1838. At that time, Robert was serving as president of the Austin County Board of Land Commissioners. Fourteen months later, they welcomed another daughter, Caroline Louise Kleberg, born on January 14, 1840. The following year, Robert became a Justice of the Peace, and in 1841, their first son, Otto Joseph Kleberg, was born on October 27. By 1846, Robert had become Chief Justice of Austin County. Rosa then gave birth to a son, Rudolph Kleberg, on June 26, 1847, who was the last of her children born in Cat Spring.[67]

After Rudolph's birth, the Kleberg family moved to Meyersville, Texas, where Robert continued his legal and political career. He was elected as one of the county commissioners in 1848 and became the DeWitt County Chief Justice in 1853. Their next son, Robert Justus Kleberg, Jr., was born on December 5, 1853, and Rosa gave birth to her last child, a daughter named Louise Rosalie Kleberg, on September 2, 1855.[68]

During the War Between the States, Robert along with his two oldest sons, Otto and Rudolph, joined the Confederate Army. Robert organized and was the Captain in command of a company named the Coleto Guards, Texas State

Troops, primarily charged with guarding the area in and around DeWitt County. Although her husband Robert remained nearby, Rosa once again found herself alone with the responsibility of raising and protecting her children.

Rosa Kleberg's youngest son, Robert Kleberg, Jr., received his early education in private schools. Following in his father's footsteps, he received a Law Degree from the University of Virginia in 1880. After receiving his Texas Law License, he started his practice in Cuero, Texas, and soon moved to Corpus Christi, where he established a law partnership with Judge John W. Stayton, Robert Stayton, and Samuel Lackey. In the summer of 1881, Robert won a lawsuit against Richard King, owner of the Santa Gertrudis Ranch (King Ranch). King was so impressed with the legal expertise of the young Kleberg that he invited him out to his ranch in hopes of hiring him. Robert later described the trip in a letter to his parents saying:

> *"Captain King had written to come out to see him and to name the day and he would meet me at the road as he lives about eighteen miles from the railroad, so I went on the railroad and found him waiting for me at the depot with his carriage. ... We had a delightful trip out to his ranch – he drove a pair of fine fast horses and in two hours we were at his ranch. ... At the ranch a table was loaded with good things to eat and drink; he lives like a prince and has a regular French cook. He treats his friends to the best he has. .... We rode all day, and he showed me his land. He has 1,000,000 acres of land. ... He wants us to attend his business for him and I hope we are to find it remunerative."* [69]

While at the King Ranch, Robert met Captain King's youngest daughter, Alice Gertrude King. After the meeting, Robert Kleberg was so impressed with Richard King and his daughter Alice that he agreed to be the principal counsel for the King Ranch. Over the next four years, the romance between Robert and Alice grew strong while the Captain's health grew weak. He died from stomach cancer on April 14, 1885.

Henrietta King inherited the massive King Ranch after her husband Richard's death. Henrietta was a strong woman and a keen businesswoman who clearly understood that with the right help, she could not only maintain the

Ranch but grow it to a new height. Henrietta chose Alice's fiancé, Richard Kleberg, to be the ranch manager. In a very short time, she proved that her choice was right. Alice King and Robert Kleber were married in the parlor of the King's home on June 17, 1886. Alice loved and adored her mother but also grew to love Robert's mother, Rosa, who she treated as family. After her husband, Robert Kleberg, Sr., died on October 30, 1888, Rosa spent most of her days and many of her nights at the King's home. Having the advantage of her very affluent background, Rosa was in charge of the elaborate social gatherings at the Ranch. After years of being an essential part of the King family, Phillipine Sophie Caroline Luise Rosalie Von Roeder Kleberg died in Meyersville, DeWitt County, Texas, on July 3, 1907.

Leaving behind the comforts of her homeland, Rosalie Kleberg embarked on a daring adventure to the untamed Texas frontier with her new husband. She was shipwrecked, left on a barren island, and later driven from her home by an Army led by an unmerciful tyrant who destroyed most of her worldly possessions. With remarkable courage and resilience, she overcame these trials and spent her final years in the company of one of the wealthiest families in Texas. Rosalie's story remains an inspiration, embodying the true spirit of a Texas woman for generations to come.

Angelina Belle Peyton Eberly
(1798 – 1860)

It was widely recognized that women in the Republic of Texas were unafraid to make use of knives and guns. One remarkable woman, Angelina Eberly, demonstrated her bravery by using a cannon. She is best known for her pivotal role in a conflict known as the *"Archives War."*

Angelin Belle Payton was born to John and Margaret Hamilton Payton in Sumner County, Tennessee, on July 2, 1798. She married her first cousin, Jonathan C. Payton, in Sumner County on July 2, 1818.[70] The couple's first child, Alexander, was born in 1820, possibly in Louisiana. In New Orleans, in 1822, the couple and their young child boarded a ship named *"Good Intent,"* bound for Matagorda Bay in the Mexican Province of Texas. They moved inland and eventually settled at San Felipe de Austin, on the Brazos River, in 1825. There, they operated an inn and tavern. The couple's second child, a daughter named Margaret, was born on October 23, 1830. Jonathan died in 1834, but Angelina kept operating the inn until the town of San Felipe was destroyed on March 29, 1836, during the *"Runaway Scrape"* as settlers were fleeing from the Mexican Army. After the Texas Revolution, Angelina was living in Columbia, Texas, where she met and married a widower, Jacob Eberly, on November 8, 1836. Jacob was a Texas Army veteran who owned land in 4 Texas Counties. After leaving Columbia, Jacob and Angelina lived briefly in Bastrop and moved to Austin in 1839. They were among the earliest settlers of the new town.

Prior to Austin being selected to be the Capital of the Republic of Texas, the area was a community known as Waterloo. It was located on the north bank of the Colorado River, near the current site of the Congress Avenue Bridge. When the Capitol of Texas was moved from Houston to Austin, Angelina quickly opened an inn that she named the Eberly House. She served dinner for President Mirabeau B. Lamar and his cabinet on October 18, 1839. When Sam Houston became President again in 1841, he preferred to stay at the Eberly House rather than the President's House. Sam Houston was staunchly opposed to the Capitol being moved to Austin. He insisted that Austin was far too remote and too close to Mexico and warring Indian tribes like the Comanches. Sam Houston insisted that Austin was *"the most unfortunate site on earth for a seat of government."*[71]

On March 5, 1842, a Mexican force of 700 men, under the command of General Rafael Vásquez, seized San Antonio. Although they withdrew 2 days later, Sam Houston took advantage of the opportunity by reasserting his demands to move the Capitol from Austin. He declared an emergency and called a special session of Congress in the city of Houston. There, he insisted that the National Archives be removed from Austin immediately. Fearing that the Capitol might be moved, the citizens of Austin formed a "*Committee of Vigilance*" to prevent the removal of the archives. Angelina's husband, Jacob, had died of yellow fever while doing business in Victoria, Texas, in 1841, but Angelina was determined to remain in Austin. On December 5, 1842, Sam Houston had re-assembled the Congress at Washington-on-the-Brazos, demanding a resolution to remove the archives from Austin. A confessed enemy of Sam Houston, Senate President Edward Burleson refused to support the resolution, and the vote stalled in a tie. On December 10, Sam Houston ordered Colonel Thomas I. Smith and Captain Eli Chandler to take 20 men, remove the archives from Austin, and return them to Washington-on-the-Brazos with "*secrecy, efficiency, and dispatch.*"

On December 30, 1842, Smith, Chandler, and their men arrived in Austin and began loading the archives. When Angelina emerged from her inn and saw what was happening, she started calling for the citizens of Austin, and a crowd quickly gathered. The city kept a cannon loaded with grapeshot on Congress Avenue near the archives building as a defense against an Indian attack. Angelina turned the cannon toward the archives building and lit the fuse. Some of the grapeshot hit the building, but there was no serious damage. However, the blast sent Smith, Chandler, and his men running with archives loaded in their wagons. By noon on New Year's Eve, a mob held the troops at gunpoint, and the archives were returned to Austin. The "*Committee of Vigilance*" celebrated the event with a New Year's party.[72]

It is uncertain why Angelina left Austin. Her son, Alexander, died somewhere between December 1842 and August 1843. Around 1846 or 1847, Angelina leased Edward Clegg's Tavern House in Lavaca (now Port Lavaca). Her daughter Margaret married James Thompson Lytle in Port Lavaca on October 26, 1848. The couple had one daughter, Peyton Bell Lytle, Born in October 1850. Margaret died on December 2, 1850. Angelina was said to have been operating a hotel in Indianola in about 1851. She died there on August 15, 1860, and was buried in a nearby cemetery. She died in the same place where she first saw Texas. Her granddaughter died in 1873 and was buried beside her, but a hurricane and flood struck the area in 1875, washing away their headstones.

Angelina Eberly's life mirrored many others who came to Texas, so very full of dreams and hopes, but twice widowed and childless, she died alone. She was a pioneer, a businesswoman, a political activist, and a symbol of the power of women in a time when such power was rarely acknowledged. Although a single explosive act proved that one person, driven by passion and conviction, can change the course of history, it was not that act that defined her legacy but rather the story of her strength and courage that remains in the hearts and minds of the generations that follow.

Chapter 4 – The State of Texas
(USA 1845 – 1861)   (CSA 1861 – 1865)

Soon after Texas gained its independence from Mexico, many of the citizens of the new Republic expressed a desire to be annexed by the United States. Several issues prevented that from happening for almost a decade. A leader among those who opposed annexation was Mirabeau B. Lamar, the second President of the Republic. He stated in his inauguration speech:

> *"I cannot regard the annexation of Texas to the American Union in any other light than as the grave of all her hopes of happiness and greatness; and if, contrary to the present aspect of affairs, the amalgamation shall hereafter take place, I shall feel that the blood of our martyred heroes had been shed in vain."* [73]

A major concern was that annexation would likely cause another war with Mexico. The Mexican government had never fully recognized Texas as an independent nation and was becoming increasingly hostile. The Texas Boundary Act of 1836, which established the Rio Grande River as the southern border of the Republic, further agitated Mexico, which considered the border to be further north, along the Nueces River.

Another consideration about annexation was the citizenship requirements for serving in the United States Congress. The U.S. Constitution required that a member of the U.S. Senate be a citizen for nine years and members of the U.S. House of Representatives be citizens for seven years.

The most significant opposition on the United States side came from those who opposed the expansion of slavery. U.S. Representative John Quincy Adams of Massachusetts was a leader in the opposition. In January 1844, a resolution, adopted by the State of Massachusetts, was sent to the U. S. Congress, saying in part,

> *"Resolved, That, under no circumstances whatsoever, can the people of Massachusetts regard the proposition to admit Texas into the Union in any other light than as dangerous to its continuance in peace, in prosperity, and in the enjoyment of those blessings which it is the object of a free Government to secure."*

Other notable U. S. leaders who opposed annexation, included Martin Van Buren, and Abraham Lincoln. While many of the other Congressmen were not particularly opposed to slavery, some of them were opposed to the further expansion of it.

Despite the issues of expanding slavery and war with Mexico, most of the United States Congressmen were in favor of annexation. On February 27, 1845, the U. S. Senate passed a bill approving Texas statehood by a vote of 27–25. The next day, the U. S. House of Representatives approved the bill by a vote of 132–76. In response, the Republic of Texas held an annexation convention on July 4, 1845, where delegates accepted annexation by a vote of 55 to 1. Three months later, the issue was put before the people, and on October 13, 1845, citizens of the Republic of Texas voted 4,245 to 267 in favor of statehood. Although international law required a treaty for one country to annex another, the Republic of Texas became the 28th U. S. State on December 29, 1845, by a joint resolution of the United States Congress. On February 19, 1846, a ceremony was held in front of the Texas Capitol in Austin, where Anson Jones, the last President of the Republic of Texas, lowered the Texas flag from the pole in front of the Capitol. The United States Flag was then raised. In his parting speech, Anson Jones proclaimed, *"The Republic of Texas is no more."*

Life for white women changed very little at the beginning of statehood, and life for Black women bound by slavery, there was no change at all because, under United States law, they were still treated as property. For Native American women, life was beginning to take a turn for the worse. They were often caught in the middle of the Texas and United States efforts to remove all native tribes from the frontier and herd them onto reservations. The reality of war would soon change life for all of them.

As everyone anticipated, tensions between the United States and Mexico, simmering since the annexation, finally boiled over. On May 13, 1846, the United States declared war against Mexico. Like any war, as the men went off to fight, women and children were left to face their own agonizing battles. Sometimes, spending months in isolation, women were the sole providers for the family. They bore the burden of protecting themselves, their children, and their homes on a frontier filled with danger. In addition to carrying those responsibilities, Hispanic women often suffered abuse due to prejudices increased by the conflict with Mexico, even those women whose fathers, sons, and husbands had fought for Texas independence.

The war lasted from May 1846 to February 1848. When it was over, more than 13,000 Americans had died, many of them from disease. More than 1,000 Texans never returned to their wives and mothers. The war officially ended with the signing of the Treaty of Guadalupe Hidalgo. Under the terms of the treaty, Mexico relinquished all claims to Texas and recognized the Rio Grande as the southern boundary with the United States. It also ceded an enormous area of land that included present-day California, Nevada, Utah, New Mexico, most of Arizona and Colorado, and parts of Oklahoma, Kansas, and Wyoming.

After the war, the State of Texas was still facing serious problems. Raids by Native American tribes were common. Despite the promise of aid from the United States, Texas was still suffering financial hardships. By 1850, the border of Texas was being challenged by the United States government. During the dispute, Texas threatened military force against the United States to defend its borders and also threatened secession. The dispute was settled as a part of the Compromise of 1850. As a condition of the Compromise, the United States paid ten million dollars to settle Texas debts and set the boundaries of Texas to what is approximately its present-day boundaries.

For the next decade, Texas grew rapidly and succeeded in building towns and roads to bring it to some resemblance of a civilized society. According to the U. S. Census Bureau, the population grew from 212,592 in 1850 to 604,215 in 1860. What had become a thriving state with a fairly peaceful existence would soon be rattled by new threats of war. Like the other Southern States, Texas depended on selling agricultural products, primarily cotton. Heavy import tariffs at southern ports were taking their toll on the economy. There were also political rivalries over the path of the new transcontinental railroad. Texas contended that it should go along the existing overland mail route to California. In addition, the newly formed and upcoming Republican party was trying to bring Kansas into the Union as a free state despite it being below the north-south dividing line, which was drawn by the Compromise of 1850. They were not opposed to and actually defended slavery in the States where it existed, but they were adamantly opposed to the expansion of slavery into the new territories. South Carolina threatened to secede from the Union, prompting other States, including Texas, to start similar discussions. Northern Democrats were divided from Southern Democrats over issues such as the path of the inter-continental railroad. Four parties emerged with their candidates in the United States Presidential Election of 1860. Northern Democrats chose Stephen A. Douglas of Illinois, Southern Democrats chose John C. Breckinridge of Kentucky, Republicans chose Abraham Lincoln of Illinois, and the Constitutional Union Party chose John Bell of Tennessee, a party that had also nominated Sam Houston. When Abraham Lincoln emerged as the winner of the 1860 election, South Carolina seceded from the Union, followed immediately by Mississippi, Florida, Alabama, Georgia, Louisiana, and Texas. By June 1861, four other states seceded.

Although shots had been fired long before Abraham Lincoln took office, he took the firing upon Fort Sumter as an opportunity to ask Congress for troops to stop what he called an insurrection. The result was the start of the deadliest war in American History. Out of nearly 90,000 Texans who entered the war, approximately 24,000 died. The war touched almost every family in Texas. In some cases, every male family member was killed.

For women, the war years were more complex than anything they had ever experienced. Sometimes, waiting years for the return of the husbands, sons, fathers, and brothers, they went about the daily tasks of protecting and providing for their children. After their return, many of the men were still seriously wounded and partially or fully disabled. In 1881, Texas set aside land for specific disabled Confederate Veterans, and by 1889, started paying pensions to those veterans who were indigent. The pensions only amounted to a few dollars, but widows could also draw a pension. In 1908, a women's home was opened in Austin for widows, wives, and orphans of Confederate veterans.

Many women never recovered from the devastation caused by the war. Black women who were former slaves often found themselves homeless and with no means of support. Native American women shared in the misery. As soon as the war was over, the U. S. Army focused on removing Native Tribes from the western frontier.

Texas was readmitted to the Union on March 30, 1870. Only then were they allowed to start governing themselves again. By the 1870s, cattle were starting to replace cotton as a major source of wealth. Ranching caused an increased urgency to remove Native Americans from the western plains. Buffalo were slaughtered by the thousands to deplete their food and clothing supply.

Many women had stories that should have been recorded during that time, but thousands have been lost to time. Of those stories that survived, they were often tales of heartbreak and grief. Others, however, are stories of courage and determination that will forever define the *"Spirit of Texas."*

Sophia Suttenfield Porter
(1815–1897)

A beautiful and flirtatious young lady, Sophia Suttenfield, left her Indiana home and arrived in Nacogdoches in 1835. She later found herself near Harrisburg just as the Battle of San Jacinto was over. Two husbands and seven years later, she was living in a mansion on the Red River, where she lived for the rest of her life.

Sophia Suttenfield was born in Allen County, Indiana, on December 3, 1815, to William and Laura Taylor Suttenfield. At the age of 17, she married Jesse Augustine Aughinbaugh on July 20, 1833.[74] By trade, Jesse was a *"sutler"* who traveled and sold provisions primarily to soldiers. By 1835, the couple had made their way to Texas and headed for the town of Nacogdoches. Somewhere along the way, Jesse abandoned Sophia. She continued heading South, with who, how, or why is unknown. She arrived at the site of the Battle of San Jacinto just after it was over. Sources claim that she tended to Sam Houston, who was injured in the battle. It is also said that Sophia became a very close friend of Sam Houston.[75] One source went on to say that Sam Houston enjoyed her company on several occasions while he was serving his first term as President of the Republic of Texas.[76]

Another friend, often in the company of Sam Houston, was a handsome young colonel named Holland Coffee. It was also reported that he was very wealthy. It may not have been love at first sight, but in a short time, Holland was also enjoying the company of Sophia. The problem was that Sophia was still legally married, so on July 25, 1838, Sophia filed for divorce in Harris County District Court. Judge James W. Robinson was reluctant to order the decree without hearing from Aughinbaugh, so the divorce was delayed for several months.

Sophia was finally granted her divorce on January 15, 1839. In Washington County, Sophia and Holland were married on February 19. Leaving the town of Independence, the couple took a long honeymoon ride which ended in Grayson County, where he had established a trading post in 1837. There, local settlers honored the couple with a grand ball.

Sophia's first home was a 100-square-foot log cabin that served as a home and a trading post. Despite her cramped living conditions, she wrote in her memoirs that she was *"the happiest woman in Texas."* By 1843, Holland had established himself as a trader and continued to acquire land and slaves. He was soon a successful planter. He built a fine mansion on his plantation that he named *"Glen Eden."* The mansion was a two-story log structure with massive stone chimneys on each end. Both the front and the back had large full-length porches on the bottom floor covered by detailed balconies on the second floor. The mansion was the center of attraction in the area and was the site of many elegant social gatherings hosted by Sophia.

Neither Holland nor Sophia had children, but they raised two of Holland's nieces. In the fall of 1846, a 28-year-old Indian agent from Fort Washita named Charles Ashton Galloway, who had recently married Holland Coffee's 14-year-old niece, accused Sophia of having an affair with another man. On October 1, 1846, Holland Coffee armed himself and went to confront Galloway. During the brawl that ensued, Galloway pulled a knife and stabbed Holland Coffee to death. Galloway was charged with murder, but a jury ruled that he was acting in self-defense.[77] Holland Coffee was buried at Glen Eden where he was entombed in an above ground crypt.

After her husband was buried, she closed the trading post and dedicated her time to managing the 3,900-acre plantation. She continued to entertain her guests at lavish social events. She was now a charming, wealthy widow and conducted herself as such. It did not take her time to cast her spell on another handsome military officer.

In February 1848, Sophia married Major George N. Butt. He was described as a man possessing exquisite southern charms, a wine expert, and handsome enough to turn the heads of most ladies. He also loved hosting social events and enjoyed partying just as much as Sophia. She immediately charged him with the responsibilities of managing the plantation. That gave Sophia time to attend to her garden. George Butt was very dedicated and efficient as a plantation manager and built a substantial cotton business at Glen Eden. In February 1863, George went to Sherman, Texas, to sell Cotton, and as he was on his way back to Glen Eden, he was ambushed and killed by a group of unknown assailants. Sophia insisted that George had been killed by soldiers of Confederate Colonel William Clarke Quantrill's raiders. While it is known that Quantrill's cavalry was camped in Grayson County around that time and that his men sometimes attacked cattle thieves who had crossed the Red River from the Indian Territory, it was never proven that they were involved in the ambush. For unknown reasons, George N. Butt was buried in Sherman, Texas, rather than Glen Eden.

During the War Between the States, Texans living along the Red River were constantly threatened by bands of outlaws, Indian raids, and sometimes Union soldiers. In early 1863, Colonel James G. Bourland, a frequent visitor to Glen Eden, organized a regiment of cavalrymen to guard and protect both sides of the border along the Red River. It was given the name Bourland's Border Regiment. The story of an event that happened during that time involving Sophia, Union soldiers, and the Border Regiment is an epic Texas folk tale. While there are several versions of the narrative, the most often-told story says that Colonel Bourland and his regiment made a brief stop at Glen Eden on their way to Fort Washita.[78] As they left, no sooner than they crossed the Red River, a group of Union scouts, in pursuit of Bouland, arrived at the plantation. Being the Southern supporter and Texas patriot that she was, Sophia devised a plan to deal with the soldiers. Rather than attempting to remove the soldiers from her property, she turned on her exquisite charm and invited the soldiers to enjoy the offerings of her extensive wine cellar. After the men had their fill of wine, Sophia treated them to a fine supper, and once supper was over, she invited them back to the wine cellar. Giving them just enough time to be over-intoxicated, Sophia locked them in the cellar and dashed to saddle a horse. She then gallantly road across the Red River and galloped across the Indian Territory to warn Bourland. After she found the regiment, they accompanied her back to Glen Eden, where they found the soldiers in a drunken state, still sampling the wine. Bourland and his men took them prisoner without a struggle. Some historians recounting her bold ride called her the *"Paul Revere of Texas."* Another, pointing out her display of Southern charm, called her the *"Scarlett O'Hara of Texas."*

There were many other unsubstantiated claims about Sophia's bravery and determination. Many of the tales proclaimed her to be a fearless Indian fighter. One story tells that Sophia had cotton bales all around that mansion, where she and her slaves defended themselves against an Indian attack. As always, once the drama was over, she went back to partying.

By the late spring of 1865, the War Between the States was over, and Sophia learned that all slaves in Texas would be emancipated. Without slaves to help operate the plantation and without a husband or family to guard against Indian attacks, she decided that she could no longer care for herself at Glen Eden. It was said that she loaded a fortune in gold coins into buckets, loaded her wagon, and moved to Waco. There, she met and married a former judge and Confederate veteran named James Porter.[79] After the marriage, the couple decided to move back to Glen Eden.

James Porter was born in Kentucky in about 1809. He became an attorney and moved to Independence, Missouri, in about 1850. There, he served one term as a judge and was a partner in the firm of Hall & Porter, which had a contract to carry mail from Independence to Santa Fe, New Mexico. When the War Between the States started, James joined the Confederate Army and served until the end of the War. He later moved to Texas.

Sophia and James lived a comfortable and happy life together until James died on September 10, 1886. Prior to his death, Sophia found religion. She became a member of the Methodist Church in Sherman, Texas, in 1869. She and James gave land for a Methodist Church near Preston Bend. The couple also donated to the denomination's college, Southwestern University in Georgetown, Texas.[80]

James Porter had been the love of Sophia's life for 21 years. After his death, she lost interest in the social activities she had been so passionate about for the 43 years that she had lived in Glen Eden. The beauty that once caused men to fight over had faded. One bright spot in her later years was her long-time friend and seamstress, Belle. She helped Sophia search the shops in Sherman and Denison for the latest fashions. If she could not find what she wanted in North Texas, she would order dozens of dresses from New Orleans or have Belle sew them for her. Sophia would have Belle dye her hair on a weekly basis to help hide the gray.[81]

Sophia Suttenfield Aughinbaugh Coffee Butt Porter died peacefully in the mansion that she had lived in for 54 years. She was laid to rest beside her husband, James Porter, in a Cemetery near Preston Bend. In August 1939, the U. S. Army Corps of Engineers began transferring the graves of the old Preston Bend Cemetery to higher ground beyond the waters of present-day

Lake Texoma. The new Preston Bend Cemetery is the final resting place for more than 700 people, including Holland Coffee, Sophia Porter, and James Porter. The plan for the Glen Eden Mansion was to rebuild the historic structure on higher ground to serve as a museum. The old mansion was dismantled, and each board was carefully numbered. What mistakenly appeared to be an old pile of lumber was burned to use for firewood thus Glen Eden was no more.[82]

Sophia Porter lived a unique and interesting life, shrouded in folklore and legend. While a part of that life included four husbands and several lovers, it also illustrates a woman who truly loved Texas. She was undoubtedly a courageous woman who contributed to the rich heritage of the Lone Star State.

Cynthia Ann Parker
(1827 – 1871)

Cynthia Ann Parker, by William Bridgers, 1861, courtesy of DeGolyer Library, SMU. Photo in the Public Domain.

Cynthia Ann Parker lived in two very different worlds. After surviving the massacre of her family, she spent half of her life as a member of the Comanche Tribe, becoming the wife of a Comanche chief and the mother of his children. In what was said to be a rescue, she was forcibly returned to a society where she no longer belonged. Deep down, her heart told her that she should be with her husband's people, but she was never allowed to go back.

Cynthia Ann Parker was born around 1827 in Illinois to Silas M. Parker and Lucinda (Lucy) Duty Parker. In the fall of 1833, Silas moved to Mexican Texas, where he had applied for a grant of one league of land near what is now Groesbeck in Limestone County. He did not receive the title to the land until April 1, 1835. His brother John and his family also settled in the area.

Silas and his brother John recognized the need for security in this hostile environment. They constructed a fort to protect their families and other settlers from attacks. The fort, a significant undertaking, featured 12-foot-high log walls enclosing an area of approximately four acres. Two corner blockhouses provided elevated vantage points for lookouts, allowing residents to spot approaching threats. Within the protective walls, six cabins were built to house the families who sought refuge within the fort.

On May 19, 1836, a party of approximately 500 to 700 Native Americans, primarily Comanches and Kiowas, appeared within a few hundred feet of the fort and approached with a white flag. There were only five men inside the fort at the time. One of the Parker brothers, 48-year-old Benjamin, went outside the fort to talk with them. Suspecting that the warriors had hostile intentions, Benjamin returned to the fort and told Silas that there was no way for five men to hold off that many Comanches and offered to go out and approach them to buy enough time to get the women and children out the back gate. Silas insisted that he would be killed and that he should stay inside the fort, but Benjamin rushed out the gate. Silas soon followed him outside, and both men were killed Instantly. When no one closed the gate, Comanches rushed in. Still inside the fort, Samuel Frost, Robert Frost, and John Parker were also killed. John's wife watched in horror as her husband was castrated and scalped. Five others were captured: Elizabeth Kellogg, 9-year-old Cynthia Parker and her 6-year-old brother John Parker, Rachel Plummer and her son James Plummer. Others were injured but managed to run through the woods and escape.[83] When the bloody fight was over, the Comanches gathered their captives and rode away.

There was a great disparity in the way that the captives were treated. Because they were so young, Cynthia and her brother John were accepted into the tribe and adopted by a Comanche family. That was not the case for her 17-year-old cousin, Rachel Plummer. She was beyond puberty and too old to be adopted, so she was treated as a slave. At one point along the journey, some of the braves decided that her young son was slowing her down and interfering with her duties as a slave, so they beat him to death and mutilated his body right in front of her.[84] Rachel was pregnant at the time of her capture. She gave birth to a second son in October 1836 and named him Luther. Once again, tribesmen decided that the child was interfering with Rachel's work and killed the infant around the age of six weeks.[85] She was ransomed out of slavery in June 1837 and reunited with her husband but arrived weak, thin, and covered with scars. She gave birth to her third child on January 4, 1839. Rachel died on March 19, 1839, and her child died two days later, just hours before Rachels' 20th birthday.[86]

Although uncomfortable, Cynthia Ann and John Parker's ride was not as brutal as that of Rachel. The two siblings had been sheltered by their mother and had not witnessed the killing of their father nor the savage murders of the others. Their trip to the village on the high plains was, for the most part, uneventful.[87]

At her new residence among the Comanche, Cynthia began learning the skills necessary to sustain life on the prairie. Under the supervision of her mentor, she learned more advanced skills, such as curing hides and making clothing items. Her younger brother was given similar tasks. After several years, Cynthia was deemed ready for marriage in about 1840. At the time, Peta Nacona was a young brave with leadership skills and the promise of becoming a war chief. He selected Cynthia Ann from among the eligible females available. He discussed his decision with Cynthia's guardian and made plans to take her to his lodge. By the simple act of taking Cynthia to his lodge, he was declaring her to be his wife. Walking behind Peta Nocona, Cynthia took the ritualistic walk to his lodge. After entering his tepee, she acknowledged her commitment to Peta Nocona and submitted herself to him in anticipation of producing a child and further committed to being his wife for life. Although Comanche men often had several wives, it appears that Cynthia was Peta's first and only wife. The couple's first child was born in 1845, and they named him *"Quanah,"* which, according to descendants, means "Sweet Aroma." A second son, named *"Pecos,"* was born in about 1849. It is believed that he died of yellow fever in about 1862. The couple's third child was a daughter born in about 1858. They named her Toh-Tsee-Ah or Topsannah, which means *"Prairie Flower."*

Peta Nocona led a band of Comanche warriors through Parker County, Texas, in early 1860. After the raid, Nocona led his warriors to a familiar place along the Pease River near Mule Creek. The raid caused residents in North Texas to demand increased protection from the State Government. Texas Governor Sam Houston commissioned Captain Lawrence Sullivan (Sul) Ross to organize a company of 40 Texas Rangers and 20 Militiamen and report to Fort Belknap in Young County. After leaving the fort, the company moved northwest toward Parker County in pursuit of the Comanches.

There are conflicting accounts concerning an event that happened on December 19, 1860, popularly known as the "Pease River Massacre." Years after the event, Quanah Parker, Comanche Chief and son of Peta Nocona and Cynthia Ann Parker, claimed that the account of Captain Sul Ross was false. He also insisted that his father, Peta Nocona, was not present at the battle and died years later. Since there were no further confirmed sightings of Peta Nocona, he was likely killed during the battle, and some of the claims made by Captain Ross may have been somewhat self-serving, but the basic facts were more than likely accurate.

In his own eyewitness account,[88] Captain Sul Ross tells that he was scouting along the Pease River when he realized that the Comanches were nearby because he saw Buffalo stampeding toward him. It was a cold and windy December day. His presence hidden by the howling wind and the dust caused by the stampede, Ross rode up on a bluff and could see a Comanche village below, that appeared to be preparing to leave. He then signaled to his men and sent 20 soldiers behind a group of sand hills to avoid an enemy retreat and then attacked from the other side with his 40 Texas Rangers. The attack was so sudden that many of the Comanche warriors were killed before they could arm themselves. When they tried to flee, they were met by the other 20 men of the company, so they began to scatter in different directions. Peta Nocona quickly rode away with a young Mexican girl mounted behind him. Holding her infant daughter, Cynthia Ann Parker was riding by his side. They were pursued by Ross and Lieutenant Tom Killiheir. After chasing them for about a mile, Killiheir caught up with Cynthia's horse and was about to shoot but stopped when she held up her child.[89] Ross continued chasing Nocona, and when he closed within 20 yards of him, he fired his pistol at the riders, believing that the Mexican girl was a man. The shot hit the girl, killing her instantly, and as she fell, she pulled Nocona from the horse with her. Instantly, Nocona began firing arrows at a rapid pace. Ross was almost dismounted when an arrow struck his horse. Ross managed to stay on and fired a shot that struck Nocona in the arm, completely disabling him. Ross then shot him twice more in the body. Holding a lance, Nocona walked a short distance away, leaned against a small tree, and began to chant. At that time, two more men rode up accompanied by a Mexican servant. He spoke Nocona's language fluently because he had once lived with the Comanche as a slave. As the Mexican translated a message from Ross to surrender, Nocona attempted to throw his lance at them. With no chance of escaping, it appeared that he would rather die than surrender. Ross directed the Mexican to end his misery with a blast from the shotgun that he was holding.

They rode back to Cynthia Ann and Killiheir and found him disgusted with himself for having run his horse so hard after a Comanche woman. After Ross looked down at Cynthia, he explained to Killiheir that she was a blue-eyed

Cynthia Ann Parker 1860-1861,
Courtesy Denver Public Library,
Public Domain

white woman, not a Comanche. Cynthia and her young daughter were escorted back to the site of Comanche village. After camping for the night, they were accompanied to Camp Cooper. Cynthia Ann cried for husband and her two sons, Quanah and Pecos, fearing that they had been killed. While at Camp Cooper, she looked for every opportunity to escape and had to be watched closely. Her uncle, a former Texas State Legislator, Isaac Parker, identified Cynthia Ann. He then took Cynthia and her daughter to his home in the town of Birdville, in Tarrant County, Texas. Parker was promised that Cynthia's two sons would be forwarded to him if they were found.[90] While Passing through Fort Worth, a photograph was taken of Cynthia Ann Parker nursing her young daughter.

Sometime in January, Parker took Cynthia Ann to Austin, where he petitioned the State of Texas for a pension and land grant for Cynthia Ann. On April 8, 1861, the Texas legislature voted to grant Cynthia a league of land and a pension of $100 per year for 5 years. They also appointed her cousins, Isaac Duke Parker and Benjamin F. Parker, guardians.

Despite being welcomed back by her biological family, Cynthia Ann never fully adapted to white society. She made several unsuccessful attempts to escape and return to her Comanche family. Separation from her Comanche family significantly impacted her mental and physical health in her last years.

In December 1863, the one shining light that still glimmered in Cynthia Ann's life went out. Her precious little "Prairie Flower" became seriously ill and died. A newspaper article reported that she was buried in the old Pilgrim Church cemetery, twelve miles from Palestine, in Anderson County, Texas.[91] Other evidence indicates that she was buried in Foster Cemetery.

For eight years, Cynthia Ann grieved the loss of her daughter while still heartbroken over being separated from her sons and the Comanche people. In March 1871, she started refusing food, gave up, and died. She was buried beside "Prairie Flower,' but that would not be their final resting place. A historical marker placed by the State of Texas in Foster Cemetery, Fosterville,

Texas, states that Cynthia Ann Parker was first buried there, and her remains were later moved to Post Oak Cemetery in Oklahoma, then finally transferred to the Fort Sill Post Cemetery. A supporting story is told by a man named Aubra Cleveland Birdsong. His first wife was Laura Neda (Ne Dah We) Parker, daughter of Quanah Parker, and they were married in Dallas, Texas, on December 7, 1904. According to A. C. Birdsong, he began working with the United States Indian Service in Oklahoma in 1906. In 1910, an act of Congress appropriated funds for the search and relocation of the remains of Cynthia Ann Parker. The Indian Department then authorized him to locate and identify her remains and have her brought back to Oklahoma for reburial. After much research, he found some people who informed him that Cynthia Ann's remains were at rest in the Old Anderson Cemetery, which is located about 4 miles South of Payer, near the Henderson and Anderson County line. On Thanksgiving Day of 1910, he learned the exact location of her remains. Two brothers, Joe and Bob Pagitt, told him they had assisted with the original burial and that Mrs. Joe Pagitt had helped prepare the body for burial. Mrs. Pagitt described in detail how she had arranged Cynthia's hair and placed a bone hairpin in it. The Pagitt brothers also stated that they had made the coffin and then gave a complete description and dimensions of it. When he unearthed the remains, he discovered everything was exactly as they had described. He also learned that the remains of her little daughter, Prairie Flower, were in the grave beside her. Although he had no authority to move the remains of the daughter, he decided to put her remains with those of Cynthia Ann and had them shipped to Cache, Oklahoma. He notified Quanah of the arrival time, and he met his mother and sister at the train station, a long-awaited reunion. After being placed in a new casket, the remains of Cynthia Ann and Prairie Flower were buried in Post Oak Mission Cemetery.

Quanah Parker was known as the last Chief of the Comanche. After his surrender on June 2, 1875, he moved to Cache, Oklahoma. Quanah invested his money wisely, and at one time, he was believed to be the wealthiest Native American in the United States. He had 5 wives and fathered 25 children. Quanah Parker died in Cache, Oklahoma, on February 23, 1911, and was buried beside his mother. In 1957, all three of the bodies were reburied in the Fort Sill Post Cemetery on what is known as Chief's Knoll.

Cynthia Ann Parker's life was a tragic symbol of the cultural displacement and loss suffered by many during this complex and often traumatic period of Texas history. Her life highlights the conflict between Native American and European cultures and the impact of westward expansion. Her enduring legacy is a blessing to the heritage of the Lone Star State.

Mary Ann Adams Maverick
(1818 – 1898)

Mary Maverick with her children. Courtesy of the Dolph Briscoe Center for American History, the University of Texas
This photo is in the Public Domain.

The word Maverick is commonly used across the southwestern United States to describe a person who is independent, and resists being branded as a member of a particular group. It originated when Samuel Augustus Maverick refused to brand his cattle, and later, the cowboys used the term to describe a cow that often strayed from the herd. When it comes to women who were independent and made their own path, the term could well describe Samuel Maverick's wife, Mary Ann.

Mary Ann Adams was born to William Lewis and Agatha Strother Lewis Adams on March 16, 1818, in Tuscaloosa County, Alabama. Both of her parents were from prominent families in Virginia. Her mother was the daughter of General Andrew Lewis, who served under George Washington during the French and Indian Wars and the American Revolution. Mary Ann was raised and educated at her parent's plantation near the town of Tuscaloosa. At 18, Mary Ann married Samuel Augustus Maverick at the home of her widowed mother in Alabama. Maverick had recently moved to the Republic of Texas.

Samuel Maverick was born in Pendleton, South Carolina, on July 28, 1803. He was raised in South Carolina but went to Yale University, where he graduated in 1825. He later moved to Winchester, Virginia, to study law and received his license in 1829. Maverick opened a law office in Pendleton but left South Carolina in 1833. He stayed for a short time in Georgia, then a plantation in Alabama, before moving to Texas in 1835. Like so many others who went to Texas, Maverick planned to build an empire there, but he arrived in San Antonio just before the *"Siege of Bexar"* and found himself in

95

the middle of the Texas Revolution. Maverick and two other men were placed under house arrest by the Mexican army and forbidden to leave the city. He was released on December 1, 1835, and he ran quickly to join forces with Benjamin R. Milam's division of Texians. After the siege, Maverick remained in San Antonio and was elected to be one of the two delegates from the city to attend the Convention of 1836 at Washington-on-the-Brazos and arrived there on March 5. He fell ill after the convention and headed back to Alabama, where he later fell in love with and married Mary Ann Adams.

After their marriage, Samuel stayed with Mary Ann at her mother's home. After a while, they started traveling around, visiting friends and family. While staying with Samuel's father in South Carolina, On May 14, 1837, the couple's first child, Samuel Maverick, Jr., was born. When their son was five months old, they headed for Texas.[92] After a short stay in Alabama, Samuel, Mary Ann, and their young child started west, accompanied by 10 slaves and Mary's brother, Robert Adams. They crossed the Sabine River into the Republic of Texas on New Year's Day in 1838, stopping later at San Augustine for wagon repairs. After several lengthy stops along the rough terrain, they reached San Antonio on June 15, 1838. Mary Ann was likely the first Anglo woman to establish a permanent residence there. On March 23, 1839, Mary Ann gave birth to another son, Lewis Antonio Maverick. He was the second of the ten children that Mary Ann would give birth to over a span of less than twenty-one years. Four of those children did not live to see their eighth birthday. It was a harsh reality of life on the frontier.

One of Mary Ann's first experiences in San Antonio was a Comanche attack. This, along with raids by bandits, was commonplace in the city. Things got worse in March 1840 as the result of an event known as the "Council House Fight," and Mary Ann was a witness. In January 1840, members of the Penateka Comanche tribe arrived in San Antonio attempting to negotiate a peace treaty. Texas officials demanded that they return all captives, leave the area, and avoid all white settlements. In response, thirty-three Penateka warriors, along with thirty-two other Comanches, arrived in town on March 19, 1840. The delegation, headed by Chief Muk-wah-ruh, brought only a few prisoners, mainly Mexican children. They also brought a sixteen-year-old White girl named Matilda Lockhart, who, along with her sister, had been captured in 1838. In the building known as the Council House, where the negotiations were being held, the girl claimed that she had been physically and sexually abused by the Comanches. Her burned, scared body and mutilated nose gave evidence to her claims. She also maintained that the Comanches still held fifteen other captives and planned to ransom them one at a time. When the Texans demanded that they release the other captives, Chief Muk-wah-ruh replied that they were being held by a different band of Comanches and that they were outside of his authority. Chief Muk-wah-ruh's explanation was rejected, and the Texans informed him and the other chiefs in the room that they were being held prisoner until the other captives were returned and Texas soldiers began entering the Council House. In response, the chiefs attempted to escape and signaled to the warriors outside for help. During the ensuing fight, thirty Penateka Comanches were killed, as well as five women and children. Seven Texans were also killed. One Comanche woman was released to go back to the other tribes and negotiate the release of the other captives, but leaders of the tribes refused.[93] That would not be the last violent encounter that Mary Ann Maverick witnessed during her Life in Texas.

The Mexican Army invaded Texas in January of 1842 and captured Goliad, Refugio, and Victoria. As they moved toward San Antonio, Mary Ann and the other women in the town began preparing their families to flee from the advancing army in an event called the *"Runaway of '42."* In September 1842, The Mexican Army arrived at San Antonio. Samuel Maverick moved his family to Gonzales County, where they stayed in a home abandoned by other settlers fleeing from the Mexican Army. Sometime later, Samuel went back to San Antonio and was one of the prisoners taken by Mexican General Adrián Woll. When the Mexican Army left San Antonio, Samuel was taken to Perote Prison in Veracruz, Mexico. He was released in April 1843, with the aid of the United States Minister to Mexica, Waddy Thompson.[94]

In 1844 The Maverick family moved to DeCrow's (Decros) Point on Matagorda Bay. Being at the entrance to Matagorda Bay from the Gulf of Mexico, the area was sometimes called Pass Cavallo (Cavallo Pass). They moved into a fine new home in April 1847. Mary Ann described the house as having eight rooms and was also three stories tall. It was very sturdy and designed to withstand strong winds. During that time, Samuel Maverick Often traveled to San Antonio, leaving Mary Ann isolated and alone with the children on the peninsula.

On October 15, 1847, Samuel and Mary Ann loaded the children and their belongings and headed back to San Antonio. The family's return to San Antonio was met by bitter cold, widespread illness, and many people suffering. Mary wrote this in her memoirs,

> "The weather grew quite cold, and we learned that many people were sick with colds and diarrhea, and almost every day somebody died, which made us quite doleful. I recalled our first residence in San Antonio, and it seemed that in those days there was scarcely any sickness and positively no case of fever, save the case of Colonel Karnes which was yellow fever imported from Houston. Now, all of our children suffered from some illness." [95]

The couple's sixth child, William Harvey Maverick, was born on Christmas Eve, 1847. The constant illness and disease surrounding everyone in San Antonio continued into 1848. On Sunday, April 30, Mary discovered that her seven-year-old daughter, Agatha, had a fever. The next day, the fever was much worse, so Mary Ann sent for the local doctor, but he could do little to help. Mary Ann spent many sleepless nights watching over her daughter. On May 9, 1848, little Agatha drew her last breath. On May 12, Mary Ann's other daughter, Augusta, also came down with a fever, from which she later recovered. Samuel, who had been away surveying land, returned on May 23. When he heard about Agatha, he went and laid down across her grave and stayed there until dark. In her Memoirs, Mary Ann told how the event had changed the lives of both her and Samuel and that she grieved the loss all her life. [96]

In April 1849, cholera struck San Antonio with a vengeance, and many died. On April 23, Augusta Maverick went to her mother complaining of stomach pains and, just after midnight, woke up violently vomiting. A doctor arrived but could do nothing. Augusta died a few hours later, just about the time that her two brothers, Lewis and John, were stricken with the same illness. Both brothers eventually recovered.

By July 1849, The Mavericks were living in a new two-story home on Alamo Plaza. Samuel and Mary Ann's seventh child, a son, was born on February 6, 1850. They named him John Hayes Maverick in honor of their friend and famed Texas Ranger, John Coffee Hayes. Baby John and his brother William were baptized on April 4 by Bishop G. W. Freeman from Louisiana. After having already lost two children so recently, Mary Ann seldom let little John out of her arms. At just five months of age, he died of Cholera on July 19, 1850.

Samuel and Mary Ann went on to have three more children. Mary Brown Maverick was born on June 17, 1851. She was the only Maverick daughter who lived to adulthood. She married Edwin Holland Terrell on August 17, 1874, and died at the United States Legation in Brussels, Belgium, on January 2, 1891, while her husband was serving as the United States Minister to Belgium. Samuel and Mary Ann's ninth child, a son simply named Albert Maverick, was born on May 7, 1854, and outlived all his siblings. He married Jane Lewis Maury on March 19, 1877. He had eleven children and died at the age of 92. Albert's story was very different from that of Samuel and Mary Ann's tenth child, Elizabeth Maverick. She was born in San Antonio, Texas, on October 17, 1857. She was a very fragile child, and in Mary Ann's words, "*a very delicate baby.*" She struggled every day of her life from her very birth. Mary Ann tried everything that she could to save her, but she died on March 28, 1859, at just 17 months of age.

When a war between the southern and northern states became imminent, Samuel struggled with the same conflicted emotions as many of his fellow Texans. Although he was born and raised in South Carolina, where the first cries for nullification and secession were made, he would have preferred that Texas did not secede. Unfortunately, it came to a point where it seemed that there was nothing else to do. When the decision was made, Samuel Maverick and his sons fulfilled their responsibilities to their beloved Texas. Mary Ann always supported her husband and their sons and loved Texas as much as they did. There is no doubt that the thought of losing yet another child was always on her mind, and now she would have to watch as hostilities unfold in front of her on the Alamo Plaza.

When the Texas Secession Convention assembled in Austin on January 28, 1861, Samuel Maverick participated as a delegate from San Antonio. After delegates voted in favor of secession, he was appointed as one of three commissioners to negotiate the surrender of U. S. Military property and forces in Texas. At the time of secession, approximately 2,700 U. S. troops were stationed in Texas and, about 100 of them in San Antonio. Major

General David Emanuel Twiggs was commander of the Texas Division, headquartered at the Alamo, which was used as a quartermaster depot for the U. S. Army. General Twiggs surrendered to Texas forces on February 16, 1861. Samuel Maverick was once again elected mayor of San Antonio in 1862 and served as Chief Justice of Bexar County, a position he held until all Confederate judges were removed after the war.

While fully mindful of the perils of war, Mary Ann stood proudly behind her sons as they volunteered for the Confederate Army. All of her sons served, with the exception of Albert, who was only eleven at war's end. Sam Jr., the oldest son, first joined Company B, First Texas Mounted Rifles, under Colonel Henry McCulloch, where he was a 1st Lieutenant. Wanting to see more action, he later joined Company G of the 8th Texas Cavalry "Terry's Texas Rangers." At Fort Donelson, Tennessee, he swam the Cumberland River and set fire to a Union Gunboat that was using hay bales for padding. For his brave actions, he was promoted to 2nd Lieutenant. He was with the regiment at General Joseph Johnston's surrender at Durham Station, North Carolina.[97] Mary Ann's second son, Lewis, was at Chapell Hill University in North Carolina when the war broke out. He first joined an Alabama regiment, but after his first enlistment period, he returned to Texas and raised a company of men for the 32nd Texas Cavalry. His brother George enlisted in Company E as a private and served with the regiment through the end of the war. Lewis was promoted in 1864 to the rank of Major in Colonel Xavier DeBray's 26th Texas Cavalry. Mary Ann's fourth son, William, was only 17 when he joined the Texas State Troops in 1865. With the exception of Lewis, all of Mary Ann's sons survived the war with only minor injuries. Lewis received a severe leg wound in 1864 that eventually crippled him; complications from his injury were a contributing factor to his early death on June 16, 1866. Mary Ann was one of the fortunate few that saw all of her sons come home from the war.[98]

By the end of the War Between the States, Samuel Maverick owned more than 278,000 acres of land, and before the end of his life, it had topped 300,000 acres. Between 1847 and 1864, he was one of the largest investors in West Texas acreage. Maverick County, on the Rio Grande south of Del Rio, was named in his honor. He was a dedicated Democrat and fought vigorously against the radical Republicans during the Reconstruction years. In 1869, his health was declining rapidly. His condition worsened in August 1870. Samuel Augustus Maverick died on September 2, 1870.[99]

Mary Ann Maverick was widowed at age 52, and her 5 remaining children were still living with her when her husband died. While she mourned Samuel's death, Mary Ann had always been a strong and independent woman, and she was little more alone than she had been over most of her 34 years of marriage. Samuel was often gone, tending to business or politics. Despite his absence, Mary Ann was a loyal and loving wife. In her memoirs, she referred to her husband as simply Mr. Maverick.

Throughout her life, Mary Ann was a very religious woman and devout Episcopalian. She played an active role in establishing St. Mark's Episcopal Church in San Antonio. After a new church, constructed of native limestone, was completed in 1875, church members gathered at Mary Ann's home near the Alamo Plaza and discovered a cannon that had been buried there during the Mexican Revolution. After unearthing the cannon, Mary Ann had it shipped to a foundry in New York, where it was cast into a bell for the new church, complete with a Texas star on the front.[100]

Mary Ann was also dedicated and passionate about preserving the history and heritage of Texas. She was a member of the San Antonio Historical Society and served as president of the Alamo Monument Association for many years. She was also a prominent member of the Daughters of the Republic of Texas. Her memoirs were an incredible account of life in early Texas.

The remarkable and inspiring life of Mary Ann Adams Maverick ended on February 24, 1898. She was buried beside her husband in San Antonio's City Cemetery No. 1. Her story was one of love, loss, and triumph. She lived on a harsh and unforgiving frontier, facing constant danger in a time when childbirth alone was a monumental feat and one that she accomplished ten times. She was a true pioneer and left an enduring legacy that continues to inspire generations of Texans.

Sarah Horton Cockrell
(1819–1892)

Sarah Horton Cockrell, Creator unknow,
Courtesy of DeGolyer Library, SMU,
Photo is in the Public Domain

Sarah Horton Cockrell is a name synonymous with the very early development of Dallas, Texas. She was a pioneer wife on the Texas frontier and also an extraordinary businesswoman. Her story reads like a thrilling adventure novel and exemplifies the *"spirit of Texas"* with her rare blend of courage, resourcefulness, and unwavering determination. Her life was a shining testament to the very best qualities of womanhood.

Sarah Horton was born in Russell County, Virginia, on January 13, 1819, to Enoch and Martha Stinson Horton. She was the fourth of seven children. In early 1844, Sarah and her family moved west, traveling in an ox-drawn wagon to Springfield, Missouri. Later that year, they arrived in the Republic of Texas and settled in the Mountain Creek area near present-day Oak Cliff in Dallas County. [101]

Alexander Cockrell, a veteran of the Mexican American War, was a neighbor of the Horton family. He settled in Texas after the war and operated a freighting business. Alexander married Sarah Horton, September 9, 1847. After the marriage, the couple built a home on Alexander's property. It was a one room log structure with a loft and a storage area. They white-washed the exterior and named it the *"White House."* Their first child, a daughter named Aurelia Effie Cockrell, was born there on May 25, 1850.

As we know it today, the city of Dallas was founded by a man named John Neely Bryan. He settled near the east bank of the Trinity River in November 1841. He was a lawyer from Tennessee and operated a ferry across the Trinity River near the site of the present-day Commerce Street Bridge. John persuaded other families to settle there, and he soon became the local postmaster. Bryan was instrumental in the creation of Dallas County in 1846. After residents voted to make the town of Dallas the permanent County Seat, he donated land for the courthouse.

For the Cockrell family, their home at the White House Ranch was getting cramped. Their second child, a son named Robert Benjamin Cockrell, was born on January 16, 1852. Soon after the birth of his son, Alexander sold his ranch, and on August 7, 1852, he bought all of John Neely Bryan's remaining property in Dallas for $7,000,[102] which included Bryan's homestead and the ferry crossing on the Trinity River. The Cockrell family moved from the White House into Bryan's five-room home in Dallas on March 21, 1853, when the sale became effective. Sarah and Alexander's third child, Ellis Cockrell, was born there in August 1863. While living in Dallas, the Cockrell enterprises encompassed several businesses, including a construction company, a sawmill, a gristmill, an office building, a freight company, and a brick company. In addition to caring for the children and managing all the household responsibilities, Sarah was responsible for bookkeeping and correspondence for these businesses. She also added to her busy schedule by giving birth to a son named Frank Marion Cockrell, born on August 29, 1854, and another son, Alexander Cockrell, born on September 6, 1856.

In 1854, Alexander established the Dallas Bridge and Causeway Company for the purpose of replacing the slow and unreliable ferry across the Trinity River. He set up a steam-powered sawmill adjacent to the construction site to improve efficiency. Workers cut down cedar trees and transported them using ox-drawn wagons to the mill for cutting. Eventually, the sawmill had to be relocated to be closer to a more abundant timber source. The new toll bridge officially opened to the public in 1858.[103] That same year, Alexander began constructing the St. Nicholas Hotel. This three-story building, which was one of the tallest structures in Dallas at the time, was situated on what is now the site of the John F. Kennedy Memorial in Dealey Plaza.

On April 3, 1858, Alexander Cockrell got into a heated argument with Dallas City Marshall Andrew M. Moore. Supposedly, Cockrell got violent when Moore accused him of violating an ordinance. Exactly what that ordinance was, is still unclear. There were rumors that the confrontation was over a debt that Moore had owed to Cockrell. The end result was that Moore shot Cockrell eight times in the abdomen. The shooting took place on Commerce

Street, near the Cockrell home. Moore was charged and tried for murder. His trial was one of the most spectacular events that Dallas had ever witnessed. After three days of trial, the jury returned a speedy verdict of not guilty.[104]

Soon after Alexander's death, the wooden bridge over the Trinity River collapsed, and Sarah was forced to re-open the ferry. In 1859, construction was completed on the St. Nicholas Hotel and soon opened under Sarah's management. On July 8, 1860, a fire devastated the town of Dallas. It was rumored to have started from a rubbish pile near a local drugstore. The fire destroyed virtually every structure in the city, including the St. Nicholas Hotel. Sarah was able to rebuild later under the name *"Dallas Hotel."* In 1860, Sarah received a charter from the State of Texas to build an iron bridge across the Trinity River, but plans for the new bridge were interrupted by the War Between the States. Little is known about Sarah's activities during the War. Her sons were too young to serve, bet her soon to be son-in-law, Mitchell Gray, was a Seargent in a Confederate Artillery Company. Knowing that she was a proud Texan, it is safe to assume that Sarah made efforts to support the Southern cause.

By 1870, Sarah had a group of new investors in the Dallas Bridge Company, but she retained a majority interest. Immediately, construction of the new iron bridge across the Trinity River was underway. Although she was the largest stockholder, Sarah did not serve on the board of directors of the Dallas Bridge Company, but her son Frank and her son-in-law, Mitchell Gray, both served on the board. Mitchell Gray's wife, Sarah's daughter and oldest child, Aurelia Effie (Cockrell) Gray, died on December 28, 1872, just nine months after her marriage. Even though Mitchell Gray remarried in 1880, he remained a part of the Cockrell family business.

At a final cost of approximately $65,000, the new iron toll bridge was opened to the public on March 2, 1872. It was 300 feet long with wooden plank decking and was 56 feet above the low water mark of the river. Dallas County purchased the bridge ten years later for $41,600 and removed the toll fees. It was in use until 1890, when Dallas County replaced it with a sturdier structure.[105] The bridge had a profound effect on the economy and population of Dallas. No longer separated from the West, in the 10 years that the Cockrell family owned the bridge, the city's population grew from about 3,000 to 10,358, and by 1890, when it was replaced, the population was over 38,000.

The bridge across the Trinity River in 1872 was an enormous accomplishment at the time, and out of all of Sarah Cockrell's achievements, it is probably the most notable. As Dallas grew, Sarah's business ventures grew with it.

Trade Mark - S. H. Cockrell & Co.
Image in the Public Domain

In the mid to late 19th century, flour milling was a major industry. In 1872, Sarah bought one-third interest in Todd Mills, the second oldest four mill in Dallas. In 1875, she bought all the remaining stock in the company and began expanding. She then formed a partnership with her son and son-in-law to form S. H. Cockrell & Company. American Beauty Mill (Standard-Tilton Flour Mill) is a successor of the Cockrell business.[106]

In the 1880s, Sarah shifted her attention to real estate. She made multiple transactions every year. Not only did she purchase property, but she sold, leased out, and rented out property. In addition to individuals, her clients included businesses, churches, and railroads. She developed the Sarah Cockrell Addition in 1884, a residential subdivision south of downtown, and in 1885, she partnered with her son Frank to construct the 5-story Cockrell Office Building. It has been said that Sarah made more than 50 separate land transactions in both 1889 and 1890 and more than 20 transactions in 1891, the year before her death. By the time of her death, Sarah owned approximately one-quarter of downtown Dallas. In addition, she owned several thousand acres in other parts of Dallas County. Her other real estate holdings include smaller tracts in Mineral Wells, Cleburne, and Houston, Texas. Sarah is also remembered for her contributions to many charitable causes, including the Methodist Church where she was a founding member.[107]

Sarah Cockrell passed away peacefully on April 26, 1892, at the home of her son Alexander. She was buried in the old Greenwood Cemetery beside her husband, Alexander, and daughter, Aurelia Effie Gray.

Sarah Horton Cockrell, a resilient pioneer woman of humble beginnings, played a significant role in the development of Dallas, Texas. Following her husband's tragic death, Sarah took the reins, demonstrating remarkable strength and business acumen with her unwavering entrepreneurial drive.

Betty Wilhelmine Holekamp
(1826–1902)

Betty Wilhelmine Holekamp
Creator unknown
Image is in the Public Domain

A German immigrant, Betty Wilhelmine Holekamp became a significant figure in the early history of Texas. Born in Hannover, Germany, she possessed a very unique upbringing, having been educated side by side with the King of Hannover's daughter. This privileged background provided her with a strong foundation in both education and social graces.

Betty Wilhelmine Abbenthern was born to Henry Christian and Marie Adelheid Roesing Abbenthern on March 4, 1826, in Hannover, Germany.[108] Betty's father became the ministerial accountant of King Ernest Augustus of Hannover. Because of her father's prominent position, Betty was allowed to be educated alongside the King's daughter. Betty also received training to become a governess.[109]

On March 17, 1844, She married Georg Friedrich "Fritz" Holekamp. Betty's husband was a royal architect and had studied music and medicine but also had practical training in farming and brickmaking.[110] On April 20, 1842, the German Emigration Company was formed by twenty-one German noblemen and was officially named Verein zum Schutze Deutscher Einwanderer in Texas (Society for the Protection of German Immigrants in Texas). The name was generally called the Adelsverein.[111] Shortly after their Marriage, Betty and Fritz Holekamp joined the immigration company led by Prince Carl of Solms-Braunfels. In September 1844, the couple left Germany along with 128 other immigrants aboard the brig *"Johann Dethardt"* bound for Texas. On November 21, 1844, they arrived in Galveston, Texas, and moved further south to Indianola. Then they moved inland toward the Texas hill country. According to the local German lore, as the colonists reached the Guadalupe River, they found the raging river swollen from recent rains. As the story goes, Prince Carl charged his horse into the river, and to the amazement of the other colonists, Betty Holekamp did the same.

Their first German settlement was given the name New Braunfels.[112] The settlement consisted of two leagues of land situated on the Comal River. It is also said that when the colonists learned that Texas had been annexed by the United States, Betty gathered scraps of cloth and fashioned a six-foot by 3-foot flag that resembled the Texas flag but had a single white star on a blue background in the upper corner and 7 red stripes running horizontally.

While in New Braunfels, Fritz Holekamp established a mill on the Comal River. He was also one of the 20 founders of a German club. The first meeting was held at the Holekamp home, and Betty served refreshments to the members. The couple's first child, George Allen Holekamp, was born there on August 7, 1846.

Prince Carl left New Braunfels soon after it was established. He was replaced as general commissioner in May 1845 by John O. Meusebach. After settling many debts, he prepared for the arrival of 4,000 new colonists. Even though the Adelsverein had received almost 4 million acres in the Fisher-Miller Land Grant, settlers were reluctant to move further west due to the threat of attacks by Native American tribes. After buying over 11,000 acres of land near the Pedernales River, Meusebach established a second colony in 1846. It was named Fredericksburg after Prince Frederick of Prussia.

Betty and Fritz Holekamp were among the first settlers of Fredericksburg. Fritz was one of the signers of the 1847 petition to create Gillespie County. When the town of Sisterdale was created later that year, the Holekamp's became the third family to move there. While living there, the couple's second child, a son named Julius Holekamp, was born on June 10, 1849.

Sisterdale was in northern Kendall County. In 1848, many Germans, known as freethinkers or forty-eighters, moved to the area. Their political views were liberalism and communism, and they were unionists during the War Between the States. One of the early residents, Baron von Westphal, was a brother-in-law of Karl Marx. Their presence in the county created a strong political divide between them and other German settlers. That divide turned deadly in 1862. There is little information about Betty and Fritz's religious or political affiliations, but Fritz did serve in the Confederate Army.

After leaving Sisterdale, Betty and Fritz moved to San Antonio. There, the couple's third child, a son named Daniel, was born on April 13, 1851, but in 1854, they were living in Comfort, Texas. The town was laid out by Ernst Hermann Altgelt. He was known to be a strong supporter of the Southern cause. Like Betty and Fritz Holekamp, many of the first settlers of Comfort had come to Texas with the Adelsverein. When liberals, freethinkers, and unionists started moving to the town, there was a noticeable political divide in the community. While living in the community, Betty Holekamp gave birth to four more children. A daughter named Dora was born on August 9, 1854; a daughter named Johanna was born on August 21, 1856; a son named Ernest was born on March 2, 1859; and the last child, a daughter named Bettie, was born on February 14, 1862.

The heated political squabble between German Unionists and those who supported the South reached a boiling point on April 16, 1862, when the Confederate Congress passed its first conscription act. Protesting the draft, a group of 61 to 68 Unionists, mostly Germans, joined forces and attempted to flee to Mexico. Led by Fritz Tegener, the Unionists camped on the west bank of the Nueces River near Fort Clark. What became known as the "*Nueces Massacre*" began when ninety-four Confederates, led by Lieutenant C. D. McRae, discovered the camp on the afternoon of August 9, 1862. Firing between the two forces started the next morning. During the battle, 19 of the unionists were killed, and 9 more were wounded. Hours after the battle, the 9 wounded men were executed. Only 2 of the Confederates were killed. Eight others were wounded, including Lieutenant McRae. Of the remaining Unionists that escaped, 8 more were killed while trying to cross into Mexico.[113] A Texas State Antiquities Landmark, Treue der Union (Loyalty to the Union) Monument was placed on High Street, between Third and Fourth, Comfort, Texas.

Sadly, Fritz Holekamp never got to see his youngest daughter. According to Confederate Military Records, he enlisted in Company B of Colonel Philip N. Luckett's Regiment, 3rd Texas Infantry at Comfort, Texas, on October 16, 1861. Without explaining if it was accidentally or deliberately, the last of his 12 records, in October 1862, shows that he shot himself and died enroute to San Antonio on September 17, 1862.[114] There is no record of his burial.

Betty Holekamp was widowed at age 36, a young age, even in that era. She came to Texas speaking only two languages, German and French, leaving her to learn English and possibly Spanish on her own. Betty was the only protection and sole provider for 6 children, ages 3 to 16, with another soon to be born. It was a dangerous time for a woman to be alone in Comfort, Texas. Most of the men in the town were off to war. It was still an untamed wilderness under the constant threat of Indian attacks and gangs of outlaws. The winters were bitterly cold, and summers were scorching hot, and the crude houses offered little protection from the elements. Diseases such as cholera and yellow fever were commonplace. Through all of the adversity, Betty was able to raise all of her 7 children to adulthood. Before her death, she was blessed with 40 grandchildren.

The 1860 U. S. Census for Kendall County lists Betty as having real estate valued at $700 and a personal estate valued at $200.[115] The 1870 U. S. Census for Kendall County lists her as having real estate valued at $600 and a personal estate valued at $400 and shows her occupation as farmer.[116] The 1880 U. S. Census for Kendall County did not list property values but showed Betty's occupation as housekeeper.[117] She last appears in the 1900 U. S. Census for Kendall County in the household of her daughter, Bettie Schmelter. The census shows that Betty aged 74, had been born in Germany in March 1826. It goes on to say that she immigrated to Texas in 1844, widowed, with 7 living children, had lived in the U. S. for 56 years, and could read, write and speak English. The census also showed that her daughter, Bettie Schmelter, was aged 38, a widowed head of the household, renting a home, and had two daughters, Natalie, aged 16, and Myrtha, aged 13, living in the household.[118] Comparing Census and Cemetery records, it appears that Bettie's son, Henry Schmelter, Jr., died before the 1900 census. Bettie Holekamp Schmelter was the last of the 7 children of Fritz and Betty Holekamp. She died in Comfort, Texas, at the age of 90 on March 7, 1952.

Betty Holekamp lived in Comfort, Texas, for another 40 years after the death of her husband. She sometimes took in boarders, and in addition to farming, she started a clothes washing and sewing business to provide for her family. Although her last 40 years were challenging, she never left the town that she had grown to love so much. She died in Comfort, Texas, on November 2, 1902, at the age of 76.

Betty Holekamp's legacy extends beyond her personal achievements. She serves as an inspiration to all who strive for a better life, reminding us of the importance of courage, resilience, and the enduring human spirit needed to overcome challenges. Her incredible story is a heartwarming reminder of the sacrifices made by the true pioneers who helped shape the history and heritage of Texas.

Sarah Ridge Pix
(1814 - 1891)

Sarah Ridge Pix (Circa 1854)
Creator unknown
Image is in the Public Domain

Born to privilege on a Georgia plantation, Sarah Ridge Pix, a raven-haired woman of Cherokee descent, became an early settler in Texas. She journeyed to the bustling port of Galveston, Texas. There, amidst the chaos of a Yellow Fever outbreak, Sarah courageously utilized her ancestral knowledge of Native American medicine to heal the sick. Trading her Galveston home for land near Trinity Bay, she forged a new path as a successful cattle rancher in Chambers County.

Sarah Ridge was born around 1814 to Major Ridge and Susannah Cathrine Wickett on the family plantation near present-day Rome, Georgia. Her father was one of the most influential men in the Cherokee Nation. His plantation, located on the Oostanaula River, featured a luxurious two-story mansion. In the 1830s, Major Ridge was regarded as the third wealthiest man in the county. His Cherokee name, which has been spelled in various ways, translates to "*The man who walks on the mountain top ridge*." In English, he was simply known as "*The Ridge*." From a young age, Ridge demonstrated exceptional skills as a warrior. Although there is no official documentation, it is said that he received the rank of Major while fighting alongside Andrew Jackson. He adopted the name Major Ridge for the remainder of his life.

Sarah lived an enviable life while on the plantation. The family mansion was adorned with elegant furniture, and the dining table was set with the finest china and silver flatware that could be found. She was fitted with a luxurious wardrobe, and the family traveled in a stylish carriage. A staff of black slaves tended to their every need.[119] Her parents wanted all of their children to be well educated, along with learning the ways of the Cherokee people. Sarah received her early education in the best missionary schools available and was converted to Christianity. Among the Cherokee, she learned their crafts and natural ways of healing and treating illnesses, including the use of herbs. In

1826, Sarah was enrolled in the Salem Female Academy in Salem, North Carolina, a seminary for young girls founded by Moravian missionaries in 1772. She completed her education there in 1829.[120]

Sarah's brother, John, and her father, Major Ridge, were prominent members of the Cherokee Council when the United States Congress passed the Indian Removal Act of 1830. They were leaders of a faction within the Council known as the *"Treaty Party."* Major, John, and others of the party signed the Treaty of New Echota on December 29, 1835. According to the terms of the treaty, the Cherokee Nation would cede its lands in the southeast in exchange for territory in the west. Although the treaty was not approved by the Cherokee National Council nor signed by Principal Chief John Ross, it was ratified in March 1836 and became the basis for the forcible removal of the Cherokee Nation. The act is historically remembered as the *"Trail of Tears,"* causing the death of approximately 4,000 Cherokees and many of its black slaves while enroute to the new territory. It also resulted in the assassination, on June 22, 1839, of Major Ridge, John Ridge, and Elias Boudinot by members of the Cherokee Nation who felt that they had been betrayed.

Colonel George Ellis Wool was a U.S. Army officer leading the Indian removal task. His aide-de-camp was a Georgia man named George Washington Paschal. Ironically, Sarah, often called Sallie, met and fell in love with George Paschal, a man who was involved in the removal of her people. They were married in East Brainerd, Tennessee, on February 23, 1837.[121]

In 1838, George and Sarah, along with the Ridge family, settled near Honey Creek in the northeastern part of the Indian Territory. It was in this new setting that they welcomed their first child, a daughter named Emily Anderson Paschal, born on May 18, 1838.[122] Following the tragic murder of Sarah's father, brother, and uncle, the couple relocated to Van Buren, Arkansas. There, George established a successful law firm. In 1842, he was elected to serve as an associate judge on the Arkansas Supreme Court; however, he resigned the following year to focus on advocating for the rights of the Cherokee Nation. On February 20, 1843, Sarah and George welcomed their third child, another daughter named Susan Agnes *"Soonie"* Paschal.[123] Unfortunately, their joy was overshadowed by the heartbreaking loss of their beloved Emily, who died at the tender age of six on November 14, 1844.[124]

Emily was buried in Mount Holly Cemetery in Little Rock, Arkansas. At the time of Emily's death, Sarah was pregnant and gave birth to a son named Ridge Watie Paschal in Van Buren, Arkansas, on July 22, 1845.[125]

In 1846, the family was temporarily staying in Washington, D.C., while George served as the legal representative for the Cherokee Nation before the United States Congress. While in the nation's capital, tragedy struck again. Their three-year-old daughter, Soonie, died on April 4, 1846, and was buried in the Congressional Cemetery in Washington D. C.[126] At the time of their daughter's death, Sarah was pregnant once more. After returning to Van Buren, Arkansas, she gave birth to a daughter named Emily Agnes Paschal, on September 23, 1847.[127]

Shortly after Emily's birth, Sarah and George moved to Galveston, Texas, bringing several slaves with them. They owned one of the first two-story houses on Galveston Island. At that time, rainwater was the only local source of fresh water, so the house included a large underground cistern.[128] Galveston Island frequently experienced outbreaks of yellow fever, and Sarah turned her home into a hospital and used her knowledge of Cherokee medicine to save the lives of many residents.

After arriving on the island, George Paschal resumed his law career and was admitted to practice before the Texas State Supreme Court on December 28, 1847. This led him to Austin, Texas, in 1850. Unfortunately, like many couples, the combination of tragic losses and long periods of separation caused Sarah and George to drift apart, resulting in their divorce on December 30, 1850. In the settlement, Sarah retained custody of their children and was awarded the house, along with several slaves. According to the 1850 U.S. Census, Sarah Paschal was a white female aged 36, and was born in the Cherokee Nation, Georgia, in 1814. Her property was valued at $2,500, and she had two sons and one daughter living in the household.[129]

After her divorce, Sarah met an Englishman named Charles C. S. Pix. The couple was married at the home of former Republic of Texas President Mirabeau Lamar in Richmond, Texas, on May 18, 1856.[130] Charles Sisson Pix was born in England to Christoper Hodgson and Matilda Gould Pix in about 1835. He appears in the 1850 U. S. Census for Galveston, with his parents and 3 siblings, and giving his age as 15.[131] He was approximately 20 years younger than Sarah. Her new husband had visions of being a plantation owner, so Sarah traded her home in Galveston to Elianor Payne "Ellen" Frankland, for 522 acres of land east side of Trinity Bay near Smith Point, in what was still Liberty County at the time. The property included a large two-story house, and Ellen Frankland's sons, Charles and Richard, were Sarah's only neighbors at the time. The couple's only son, Charles Forest Pix, was born on July 24, 1857. Family history tells that Sarah's daughter, Agnes, idolized her little brother and was responsible for giving him the name Forest.[132]

By 1860, Sarah's oldest son, George Walter Paschal, had moved to Austin to live with his father. During the War Between the States, he became a Lieutenant Colonel in the 2nd U. S. Texas Cavalry, one of the few Union Regiments ever organized from residents of Texas. His regiment was defeated by Confederate forces in the last battle of the war, the Battle of Palmito Ranch, near Brownsville, Texas. He died in Washington D. C. on February 24, 1918, and was buried in Arlington National Cemetery.[133] His brother, Ridge Watie Paschal, served two terms as Mayor of Tahlequah, Oklahoma, capital of the Cherokee Nation. He died on February 2, 1907, and was buried in Tahlequah Cemetery, Cherokee County, Oklahoma.[134]

An unconfirmed yet sad family story tells that at the age of 17, Charles Forest Pix, the only son of Charles and Sarah Pix, contracted malaria and died in Galveston on November 13, 1874. His body was shipped to Sarah in a wagon, but her husband would not allow her to bury their child on the property. His remains were left covered in the wagon for a year. Eventually, Sarah was able to bury her son near an oak tree that he had planted as an acorn.[135]

Another family story tells that Charles Pix abandoned Sara for 13-year-old Emma L. Dick. Yielding to the demands of her daughter Agnes, Sarah filed for Divorce. After some heated litigation and an appeal, the divorce was granted in September 1880. In the final decree, the judge ruled Charles Pix would leave the marriage with the same $19 that he brought into it.[136] After the divorce, Charles went on to marry Emma Dick, a marriage that produced three children. Charles died on September 8, 1900, along with thousands of others in Galveston, stricken by the deadliest storm in American History.

Sarah continued on with her ranching business. She is said to have registered a cattle brand in the shape of a lizard. The same brand that was used by her father, Major Ridge, at his plantation in Georgia.[137] Sarah Ridge Paschal Pix died on her ranch in Smith Point, Texas, on January 8, 1891, and was buried in the McNeir Cemetery, nearby.

Sarah Ridge, the daughter of the influential Cherokee leader Major Ridge, witnessed firsthand the forced removal of her people during the "*Trail of Tears*." Ironically, she fell in love with George Paschal, an aide to the U.S. Army officer who oversaw the removal. Despite bearing his children and enduring the tragic deaths of her father, brother, and two young daughters, her marriage ultimately fell apart under the weight of loss and separation. Later betrayed by another husband and haunted by the ghosts of her past, Sarah remained a woman of strength and resilience. She rebuilt her life as a successful rancher in Texas, leaving behind a legacy that intertwines with both the triumphs and tragedies of her remarkable life.

Elizabeth "Bettie" Munn Gay
(1836–1921)

Elizabeth "Bettie Munn Gay
Creator unknown
Image is in the Public Domain

Unlike many Texas Women of the nineteenth century who were confined to the domestic sphere, Bettie Munn Gay, was a whirlwind of unyielding spirit who dared to storm beyond the prescribed boundaries of womanhood. Embracing the values of equality and progressiveness, she became one of the most prominent rights activists of her day.

Elizabeth Munn was born to Neill and Mary Ann Talbert Munn in Monroe County, Alabama, on December 24, 1836. As a young child, she and her family immigrated to Fayette County, Republic of Texas in 1840. Elizabeth, or "Bettie" as she was called, was only five years old when her father died on November 20, 1842. Her mother, Mary Ann, bravely carried on, marrying Reddin Andrews in 1845. It is unclear how much land Neill Munn was originally granted when he came to Texas, but Title Abstract records indicate that the heirs of Neill Munn patented 257 acres in Fayette County on July 30, 1850.[138]

Bettie, a spirited farm girl, grew up immersed in the rhythms of rural life on the family land. At the tender age of fourteen, she married a much older man named Rufus King Gay. The couple's first child, a son named James Jehu Bates Gay, was born on October 19, 1856. A second child, a son named Willis Gay, was born about 1859 but died as an infant. No records of death or burial have been found. The memory of their lost child undoubtedly cast a long shadow over their lives.

With the arrival of the War Between the States, Rufus Gay enlisted in the Confederate Army. He first served for six months defending Galveston Island as a private in Company B of Colonel Ebenezer B. Nichols' 9th Texas Infantry. After 6 months in Galveston, he was transferred to Captain J. M. Finney's

Company, 3rd Battalion, Texas Volunteer Infantry.[139] After the war, Bettie and Rufus, along with their only surviving son, moved to Colorado County, where they reportedly owned a 1,700-acre farm.[140] Rufus King Gay, died in Colorado County, Texas, on April 6, 1880, leaving Bettie a widow, with a farm to manage and a mortgage to pay.[141]

After the death of her husband, Bettie became heavily involved with the Southern Farmers' Alliance, an organization created to address the economic issues of farmers. Bettie was one of the 600 delegates at the 1885 Alliance Convention in Texas, and in 1892, she was a delegate from Texas to the National Farmers' Alliance and Industrial Union meeting in St. Louis, Missouri.

Bettie, in addition to her years of support for Texas farmers, developed a passion for various other causes. She began writing articles highlighting the significant contributions of women in the Farmer's Alliance. As she explored the complexities of the Alliance, she recognized that women's invaluable efforts were often overlooked. This realization ignited a newfound passion within her, strengthening her unwavering support for the women's suffrage movement.

As she became a devoted Baptist, her faith became intertwined with her activism, driving her to passionately advocate for temperance. She believed that alcohol consumption was a scourge on society, undermining families and hindering progress. However, her activism went beyond the boundaries of religious doctrine. Bettie developed a strong belief in the intellectual superiority of women in matters of politics and economics. She firmly asserted that women, through their experiences in managing farms and households and raising families, possessed a unique and invaluable perspective on social and economic issues.

With unwavering conviction, Bettie urged women to rise up, to break free from the shackles of disenfranchisement, and to use their voices in the political arena. She envisioned a future where women would reform national policies, guided by their wisdom and compassion to lead the nation toward a brighter tomorrow.

In what might seem contradictory, Bettie developed an interest in the political philosophy known as "*Christian Socialism*," which gained popularity in the late nineteenth century. Christian socialism is the belief that Christian principles, such as love, compassion, and social justice, require the adoption of socialist economic and political systems. Francis Bellamy, the author of the Pledge of Allegiance to the United States Flag, was a notable figure in this movement.

Elizabeth "Bettie" Munn Gay's transformation from a Southern farmgirl to a political activist stands out from the typical life story of women in early Texas. Regardless of differing opinions, her impact on the "*Spirit of Texas*" was significant. As she navigated the challenges faced by Texas farmers, she embraced the Populist movement and became a strong advocate for women's rights. Bettie's Christian faith merged with her political beliefs, leading her to support the temperance movement and to explore the principles of Christian Socialism. Her remarkable journey concluded with her passing in Colorado County, Texas, on June 2, 1921.

Chapter 5 - The Texas Frontier
(1865 – 1890)

The "*Wild West*" was a turbulent era that spanned just a quarter century across the frontier of Texas, yet it has ignited the imaginations of storytellers for generations. This period is arguably the most celebrated in the history of the Lone Star State. It gave birth to a unique culture shaped by the forces of expansion. Ranchers rode alongside hardened cowboys, their weathered faces marked by the dust of the trail. Trail drivers pushed cattle north along rough roads, sharing the landscape with buffalo hunters across the vast plains. Gamblers, their eyes gleaming with greed and desperation, along with outlaws, faced off against lawmen who struggled to maintain peace in a chaotic world. Amidst this male-dominated environment emerged a new breed of fierce and independent women who defied social barriers and carved their own paths in this untamed frontier.

This period in Texas' history began at the end of the War Between the States. Virtually everyone in the state was adversely affected by the War, and many were absolutely devastated. Few women escaped the heartbreak of losing a father, brother, husband, or son. In some cases, entire families were wiped out. No race was exempted from the scourge of war. The state was placed under martial law until it was readmitted to the Union on March 30, 1870. Although cotton was still an important product, many of the farms failed during the reconstruction years. Men were forced to seek new jobs and learn new skills. The growing cattle industry became a viable solution for those seeking a new way of life. Some property owners were forced out by the unscrupulous actions of some opportunists coming to Texas seeking to exploit the state's vulnerabilities. Communities rallied together, neighbors supporting neighbors, as they collectively sought to rebuild and forge a brighter future for themselves and their families.

Many black families were suddenly homeless, reverting to camping under bridges, squatting on abandoned land, or land belonging to the State's school trust. Eventually, some of the black families were able to rent land as sharecroppers, but tensions ran high between the black and white races, often because of policies made by the provisional government placed in control of Texas by radical reformists. There is no doubt that many black women led brave and courageous lives as slaves and during reconstruction years, but due primarily to a lack of education, many of the stories were never written. Years later, a large number of oral histories were recorded, which had sometimes been handed down through their families but without reliable verification.

Despite the turmoil of the war, both sides continued their efforts to remove Native Americans from the Texas frontier. In the wake of Reconstruction, a significant influx of white and Hispanic families poured into an area of Texas previously dominated by various Native American tribes. This surge of settlers in the West was met with hostile resistance, highlighting the clash of cultures and the struggle for survival. In the Native American culture, women were equally as much a part of the struggle as were men, especially among the Comanche.

Comanche women were pivotal to their society. Their duties included raising children, gathering food, preparing meals, and crafting clothing, but their influence extended far beyond these tasks. They also played a crucial role in social and religious ceremonies. Well respected for their wisdom, Comanche women played essential roles in the Comanche decision-making process. On occasion, they fought alongside the men as warriors. Comanche people, like many other Native American tribes, did not have a written language. Their rich oral traditions passed down through generations, holding countless stories of bravery and resilience. Though much of their history remains shrouded in the mists of time, we can still honor the remarkable women of the Comanche Nation. Their courage, their strength, and their contributions to the heritage and history of Texas should be remembered and celebrated, even if only through the fragments of their stories that have survived.

If there was ever a silver lining to our nation's deadliest War, it would be the contribution of the War Between the States to the Texas cattle industry. Left by the Spanish, Texas had an abundance of free-roaming Longhorn cattle in the early nineteenth century. While several large cattle ranches were already operating in South Texas by the mid-nineteenth century, Anglo ranchers like Richard King in South Texas and Daniel Waggoner in North Texas established their own successful cattle ranches in the 1850s.

When the War Between the States began, thousands of men enlisted in the Confederate Army, leaving their cattle to roam freely with no one to manage them, which allowed the herds to reproduce unchecked. Additionally, the Union Navy blockaded Texas ports and the Mississippi River, cutting Texas cattlemen off from major markets. By the end of the War in 1865, it is estimated that over 5 million head of cattle were roaming the prairies of Texas. Meanwhile, Northern cities such as Chicago had built large meat processing plants to supply the Union Army, creating a ready market for Texas cattle. The only challenge that remained was figuring out how to transport the cattle to these markets. The first major cattle trail was the Shawnee Trail, which originated before the Civil War and ran from Texas to Missouri. However, it ultimately failed when farmers blocked the trail due to cattle infected with a deadly disease known as Texas Fever.

In June 1866, Charles Goodnight and Oliver Loving partnered in a cattle drive to transport 2,000 head of cattle from Fort Belknap in Texas to Fort Sumner, New Mexico. This route became known as the Goodnight-Loving Trail, which was later extended to Denver, Colorado, and into Wyoming.

Jessie Chisholm established a trail from San Antonio to Abilene, Kansas, around 1867, drawing cattle from as far away as the Rio Grande Valley. Although he did not live to see it named in his honor, the Chisholm Trail became the busiest and best-known trail of its time. This chapter also includes the biographies of several early Texas women who became cattle ranchers and trail drivers.

During the late nineteenth century, an estimated 55,000 cowboys rode the cattle trails. The days were long, and towns were few. When the cowboys rode into town, they were looking for alcohol, gambling, and women. Every major town, from Houston to El Paso and San Antonio to Fort Worth, had its share of saloons, gambling halls, and brothels.

Fort Worth was centrally located between South Texas and Abilene, Kansas, along the Chisholm Trail, and was the last stop before crossing the Red River into Indian Territory. This created the perfect environment for a rowdy district known as *"Hell's Half Acre."* In addition to cowboys, this area attracted various characters, from gamblers to outlaws to soldiers, who were easily separated from their money in the numerous saloons and brothels.

The women of the brothels had a significant impact on the culture of frontier Texas, both positively and negatively. The madams who owned and managed these establishments often influenced local politicians and were sometimes very successful businesswomen. While the women working in the brothels were usually cared for, it is important to acknowledge the grim reality that they were often treated as tools of the trade. Other unique women of the Texas frontier included saloon and dance hall performers, skilled gamblers, and occasionally gunfighters. These women were a special breed, learning to survive and thrive in a harsh and dangerous environment.

Just west of Fort Worth, on the Clear Fork of the Brazos River, was the town of Fort Griffin. It was a lawless frontier outpost and was pretty much the divider between Texans and the Native American Tribes of the west. It was often visited by some of the most notable lawmen, gunfighters, and outlaws in Western history, with names like Doc Holiday, Wyatt Earp, and John Wesley Hardin. It was known for the women of its saloons and dance halls, including the infamous gambler, Lottie Deno.

After the surrender of the Comanche Chief Quanah Parker and other tribes in the mid-1870s, settlers migrated west and into the Texas Panhandle. Hunters killed Buffalo at a rate that brought them to near extinction. By 1890, railroads in Texas had eliminated the need for cattle drives, and barbed wire closed the open plains.

Some of the most prominent women of the Frontier era were cattle ranchers, and a few were former trail drivers. While a breed apart from other early women of early Texas, they had the same courage and determination. Like so many others, they suffered tragic losses but had the resilience to triumph in the end, writing their own story in the history of Texas.

Margaret Heffernan Borland
(1824–1873)

Margaret Heffernan Borland
Creator unknown
Courtesy University of Texas at San Antonio
Image is in the Public Domain

Margaret Heffernan Borland, a frontier pioneer, blazed a trail across early Texas unlike any other. This indomitable woman, a ranch owner and cattle baron, fearlessly led a herd of Texas Longhorn cattle up the long and dusty Chisholm Trail. Borland's courage and resilience shattered the boundaries of gender, by proving that women could conquer the Wild West. Her remarkable feat solidified her place in history as the only woman to lead her own cattle drive, earning her the rightful title of "Cattle Queen."

Margaret Eva Heffernan was born in Ireland, to John and Margaret Ryan Heffernan, on April 3, 1824. Margaret, her parents, and two older sisters, immigrated to New York, on August 9, 1826. Her brother John Martin Heffernan was born there that same year. In 1828, two Irishmen, John McMullen and James McGloin contracted with the Mexican Government to establish an empresario colony in Mexican Texas. The contract called for settling 200 Irish Catholic families on the bank of the Nueces River. In 1829, McMullen and McGloin traveled to New York to recruit recently arrived Irish immigrants who were not established there. Two ships, the *"Albion"* and the *"New Packet,"* loaded their settlers and set sail for Texas. Arriving on the Texas Coast, the *"Albion"* mistakenly landed at Matagorda, but the *"New Packet"* landed as planned at the Port of Aransas, with John Heffernan and family aboard.[142]

By 1832, John had settled his family at San Patricia near Refugio. A son, James Heffernan, was born there the same year. In 1836, the family found themselves in the middle of the Texas Revolution. John and his brother James had planned to join Colonel Fannin's regiment, but just days before leaving for Goliad, John, his brother James, and cousin John Ryan were killed by Indians who later killed James' wife and five children.[143]

On August 16, 1843, Margaret Heffernan married Harrison Dunbar, in the town of Victoria. Little is known about Harrison Dunbar other than that he was killed in Victoria during an argument in 1844. Their daughter, Mary Dunbar was born after Harrison's death that same year.

Margaret married Milton Hardy in Victoria, Texas, on October 16, 1845.[144] The couple established a successful cattle ranch on their combined properties of 2,912 acres. The marriage of Margaret and Milton was blessed with the birth of 4 daughters and 1 son. While the exact dates of their births are unknown, their names and birth years were daughter Eliza Hardy, born 1847; daughter Julia Hardy, born 1848; daughter Rosa Hardy, born 1851; and son William Hardy, born 1852. Milton Hardy contracted Cholera and died August 24, 1855, and sadly, their infant son Willie died of the same disease. The death of her husband left Margaret a 28-year-old widow with 5 children. Her oldest child, being just 11 years of age, Margaret, had the monumental task of managing a large cattle ranch alone, so her 20-year-old brother James moved in with her to help out.

On February 11, 1856, Margaret married 39-year-old Alexander Borland. Alexander was said to be a wealthy man from the east coast. The couple increased their wealth in the cattle business. 1860 United States Census for Victoria County showed that Alexander owned real estate valued at $14,500 and personal estate valued at $28,000. It also showed that he owned 12 slaves.[145] The War Between the States gave an added boost to Margaret and Alexander's thriving cattle business. With thousands of Texans gone to the Confederate Army, they could pick and choose from the millions of cattle roaming free in Texas. It is estimated that they owned more than 8,000 cows before the end of the war.

The marriage of Margaret and Alexander produced 4 children. A son, James Alexander Borland, was born in 1856; a son, Andrew Borland, was born in 1859; a daughter, Nellie Borland, was born in early 1861; and a son, Willie Borland, was born at the end of the same year.[146]

After the War, 1866 was a happy and prosperous year for the Borland family. Margaret's daughter, Julia Hardy, married Victor Marion Rose on March 5, 1866, and was soon pregnant with her first child. Julia's husband, Victor Rose, was the son of John Washington Rose, a former Judge, State Representative, and the fifth wealthiest man in Victoria County. During the War Between the States, Victor Rose served as a Sergeant in the Third Texas Cavalry of the Confederate Army.[147] Yet another happy moment, Margaret's oldest daughter, Mary Dunbar, married Alfred Brown Peticolas on May 3, 1866, and was soon expecting her first child. During the War, Mary's husband Alfred served as a Sergeant in the Fourth Texas Mounted Volunteers.[148]

Although 1866 brought joy and happiness to the Bourland family, it marked the beginning of some of the most horrific tragedies imaginable. It was as if fate, or perhaps the cruel hand of circumstance, was casting a veil of grief over Margaret and her entire family. In 1867, Alexander fell ill and traveled to New Orleans, seeking the best possible medical treatment. His departure, however, initiated a chain of devastating losses. Back home, five-year-old Willie also became ill. While receiving treatment in New Orleans, Alexander was diagnosed with cholera. Despite the dedicated efforts of the attending doctors, Alexander passed away on March 23, 1867. Sadly, his infant son, Willie, died in Victoria a short time later.

But the tragedies did not end there. A terrifying epidemic of yellow fever swept through Victoria County, leaving a trail of sickness and death in its wake. Amidst this growing crisis, Margaret's daughter, Julia Hardy Rose, gave birth to a precious baby girl, Julia Rosa Victoria Rose, in April 1867. Just months after bringing her daughter into the world, Julia succumbed to the ravages of yellow fever in April 1867. The relentless wave of sorrow continued as both of Julia's sisters, Eliza and Rosa Hardy, also fell victim to the same merciless disease. Yet just as heartbreaking, Margaret's oldest daughter, Mary Dunbar Peticolas, gave birth to a son, Malcolm Peticolas, in September 1867. Sadly, both Mary and her newborn died from yellow fever shortly afterward.[149] It would be hard to imagine the grief and pain that Margaret must have been feeling from losing her husband, a son, 4 daughters, and a grandson, all in less than one year.

Undeterred by her grief, Margaret took the reins and proved that she was a skilled rancher and good businesswoman. She had learned from her mother that you don't have time to mourn when you are responsible for operating a ranch. She hired cowboys to do the hard work, then started buying and selling cattle and increased her herd to over 10,000 head. Her two sons were getting old enough to learn the cattle business, and her nephew John McClain Heffernan was working on the ranch with her. She also became a licensed butcher and sold her beef locally. Her skills and determination were unmatched by ranchers in South Texas. Her granddaughter, Julia Rose, lived on the ranch while her father, Victor, applied his efforts to editing and publishing the Victoria Advocate newspaper. Victor describes his mother-in-law as:

> "...a woman of resolute will, and self-reliance, yet she was not one of the kindest mothers. She had, unaided, acquired a good education, her manners were lady-like, and when fortune smiled upon her at last in a pecuniary sense, she was as perfectly at home in the drawing room of the cultured as if refinement had engrafted its polishing touches upon her mind in maidenhood."

The winter of 1871-1872 brought record cold, with snow and freezing rain, to South Texas. The freezing weather and lack of forage killed thousands of cows, and ranchers were forced to sell their herds at low prices. Margaret was selling cattle at the San Antonio market for $8.00 per head but learned that cattle were selling for almost $24.00 per head in Kansas. Margaret decided to drive a herd of cattle up the Chisholm Trail to Wichita, but rather than hire a trail boss, she would lead the drive herself.

In the spring of 1873, with no one to care for her children, Margaret loaded up her 16 and 13-year-old sons, 8-year-old daughter, and 5-year-old granddaughter and prepared to hit the dusty trail. With a group of trail hands and about 2,500 heads of cattle, they drove the Chisholm Trail to Kansas. When they arrived in Wichita two months later, local residents were amazed at Margaret's remarkable feat. While in Wichita, and before she was able to sell her herd, they discovered that Margaret had developed a brain disease known as "*Trail Fever*," sometimes referred to as "*congestion of the brain*." Margaret Heffernan Borland died in Wichita, Kansas, on July 5, 1873. After her death, her two sons were responsible for selling the herd, and after doing so, they loaded up Margaret's body and took the long trail back to their ranch. She was later buried in Evergreen Cemetery, Victoria, Texas.[150]

Margaret Heffernan Borland, an Irish immigrant, demonstrated remarkable resilience and business acumen in the challenging environment of early Texas. Following the death of her husband, Alexander, she took over the management of their Victoria County ranch, defying societal expectations and proving herself a capable cattlewoman. Borland expanded her holdings, improved cattle breeds, and implemented innovative ranching techniques, becoming a respected figure in the Texas cattle industry. Her success stemmed from a combination of hard work, shrewd negotiation skills, and a deep understanding of the land and livestock. Despite personal tragedies, including the loss of her husband and several children, Borland persevered, building a legacy as a pioneering woman in the development of the Texas ranching industry. It is truly a great story of a great Texas woman.

Henrietta Chamberlain King
(1832–1925)

Henrietta Chamberlain King
Creator Unknown
Image is in the Public Domain

Henrietta Chamberlain King, a name synonymous with the vast King Ranch, stands as a towering figure in Texas history. More than just the wife of a legendary rancher, Henrietta proved to be a remarkable businesswoman, a compassionate philanthropist, and a pivotal force in shaping the destiny of one of the world's largest and most iconic ranches.

Henrietta Maria Morse Chamberlain was born to Hiram and Maria Morse Chamberlain in Boonville, Cooper County, Missouri, on July 21, 1832. Her father was a prominent and dedicated Presbyterian minister. Her mother died at Franklin, Howard County, Missouri, on March 24, 1835.

As a result of her mother's death and her father's traveling missionary work, Henrietta's formative years were often lonely, causing her to be withdrawn and often in need of her siblings affections, but she eventually learned to be independent and self-sufficient. In about 1846, she attended the Holly Springs Female Institute in Mississippi for two years before the family headed for Texas.[151]

In approximately 1849, Henrietta and her family arrived in Brownsville, Texas, embarking on a new journey. Here, Hiram Chamberlain, a devoted man of God, established a Presbyterian Mission. Unable to find suitable housing in Brownsville, Hiram rented a vessel at the dock to serve as a temporary home. As fate would have it, It was at this very dock, where a young and ambitious ship pilot named Richard King moored his freighter. The unexpected meeting between Henrietta Chamberlain and Richard King marked the beginning of a remarkable story in their lives and the dawn of an incredible chapter in Texas history.[152]

137

Richard King was born in New York to Irish parents on July 10, 1824. His parents died, leaving Richard an orphan at age 5, and was forced to live with his aunt. At the age of 11, he secretly stowed aboard a ship bound for Mobile, Alabama. After the captain discovered Richard, he decided to keep him as a "*cabin cub*" and taught him to navigate the rivers of Alabama. By age 16, Richard was a skilled boat pilot and made his way to Florida, where he met and established a lasting friendship with Mifflin Kenedy. During the Mexican-American War, Mifflin contracted to haul supplies for the U. S. Military. He stayed in Brownsville after the War and sent a message to his friend Richard King asking him to join him in Texas.

It is unknown how long Henrietta, and her family lived at the port. We only know that she met Richard King there. Despite having totally opposite lifestyles, Richard took an interest in Henrietta. She did not drink or dance and was a refined, educated lady. Richard, on the other hand, was a hard-living, hard-drinking man who identified well with the old phrase, "*cusses like a sailor*." It was said that Richard made some adjustments to his lifestyle and even made occasional visits to the church. However, it is possible that he was using a quest for salvation as an excuse to spend time with his lady. Regardless of their differences, the relationship continued to blossom.[153]

An unyielding entrepreneur, Richard began speculating in large tracts of real estate. In 1853, he purchased the 15,500-acre Rincón de Santa Gertrudis grant, in the Nueces Strip, and in 1854, he acquired the 53,000-acre Santa Gertrudis de la Garza grant.[154] While Richard was attending his many business ventures, Henrietta was teaching at the Rio Grande Female Institute. Taking a break from their busy schedules, Richard and Henrietta were married in Brownsville on December 10, 1854. Their new home was the Santa Gertrudis Ranch. The original house was made from upright poles covered with mud, but it was later replaced with a better wood framed house overlooking Santa Gertrudis Creek.[155]

On April 17, 1856, Henrietta King gave birth to a daughter, Henrietta Maria "*Nettie*" King. Two years later, a second daughter, Ella Morse King, was born on April 13, 1858, and Henrietta gave birth to her first son on July 15, 1860. The family continued to grow as Richard and Henrietta's fourth child, a daughter named Alice Gertrude King, was born on April 29, 1862.

Richard King made a substantial portion of his immense fortune during the War Between the States. The Union Navy had blockaded all of the vital southern ports early in the War, and when the City of Vicksburg, Mississippi, fell to Union forces on July 4, 1863, the Mississippi River was in complete control of the Union Navy. Richard and his partners cleverly placed their steamboats under Mexican registry and moved their base of operations to Matamoros, giving them a greater ability to bypass the Union Blockade. When Cotton became the Confederacy's major source of revenue, the King Ranch became an official receiving station for Cotton. Richard and his partners masterfully funneled vast quantities of Cotton into Mexico in exchange for supplies and munitions for the Confederate Army.[156] In late 1863, the Union Army captured Padre Island and Brownsville. Then they moved inland in an attempt to disrupt the flow of Cotton. Although they were soon driven from the Texas Coast, they were able to make it to the King Ranch. On about December 20, 1863, Richard King was warned that the U. S. Cavalry was headed to his ranch, planning to take him prisoner. Richard decided to escape to Mexico. Since his wife Henrietta was 7 months pregnant, he believed she and the children were safer at the ranch house under the care of her father, Hiram Chamberlain, and his trusted friend, Francisco Alvarado. On December 23, 1863, a detachment of 80 U. S. Cavalrymen under the Command of Captain James Speed decided to give the occupants of the King Ranch, an early Christmas present by storming through the front gate, looting, and pillaging. Upon entering the ranch house, Speed warned Hiram Chamberlain:

> *"You tell King that if one bale of cotton is carried away from here or burned, I will hold him responsible with his life."*[157]

As soldiers began to destroy the house, a scuffle commenced and the loyal ranch hand, Francisco Alvarado, was shot to death. After causing as much damage as possible, the cavalrymen rustled some cattle and rode back to Brownsville. With the house in shambles, Henrietta loaded up his children and relocated to San Patricio, where her son, Robert E. Lee King was born on February 22, 1864. In Mexico, the defiant Richard King, continued to operate his business there.

After Union forces were removed from Texas in 1864, Richard returned to the King Ranch and re-established his business there and continued to amass his fortune until the end of the War. The end of the War created a new problem. When the United States took control of the Texas Government, their policies were enforced with a vengeance. Richard King was now a wanted man, subject to prosecution, and once again was forced to flee to Mexico. Over the years Henrietta had discovered, like many other women of early Texas, being married to a prominent successful man, included many lonely days of isolation and Richard's trip to Mexico was not the first nor would it be the last time that she would have to take full responsibility for the family. In late 1865, like several other Texans during the reconstruction era, Richard was given a pardon by President Andrew Johnson, allowing him to go back to his home and family.

In 1868, Richard dissolved his long-standing partnership with Mifflin Kenedy and became the sole-proprietor of the massive Santa Gertrudis Ranch. Although Henrietta was busy raising their 5 children, she was still heavily involved with the day-to-day business of the Ranch. Between 1869 and 1884, the Ranch sent more than 100,000 head of cattle up the dusty trails to Northern markets and at the time of Richard's death, the Santa Gertrudis Ranch was more than 825,000 acres. In April 1885, Richard King was seriously ill and suffering from the effects of stomach cancer. He traveled to San Antonio, Texas seeking medical treatment. He died there at the Menger Hotel, on April 14, 1885. The last instructions that he gave to his attorney were, "*Not to let a foot of dear old Santa Gertrudis get away.*"[158]

During Richard's last days and through the ordeal of his death, Henrietta's dearest friend and closest confidant, was her daughter, Alice Gertrude King. A brilliant woman, Henrietta knew that in order successfully operate any business, you had to surround yourself with good people. She turned over management of the Ranch to Robert Justus Kleberg II, who in addition to being the family attorney, was the fiancé of her loving daughter, Alice. Robert Kleberg and Alice Gertrude King were married in the parlor of the Santa Gertrudis on June 17, 1886. Mifflin Kenedy stood in for his old friend Richard King and gave the bride away. When the couple had their first child, on November 18, 1887, they named him Richard Mifflin Kleberg, in honor of both Alice's father and his old friend Mifflin Kenedy.[159]

In a short time, Robert Kleberg proved that Henrietta had made the right decision by making him Ranch Manager. When Henrietta inherited the Ranch, it had about $500,000 in debt but within a few years the Ranch was almost debt free and at the time of Henrietta's death in 1925, the Ranch totaled almost 1.2 million acres. Before her death, Henrietta gifted the main headquarters of the Santa Gertrudis, including the Main House and its 30,000 acres, to her daughter Alice saying she had, *"lovingly and faithfully devoted practically her whole life to my care, consolation and aid."* [160]

Henrietta Maria Morse Chamberlain King, died at the Santa Gertrudis Ranch on March 31, 1925. During her funeral procession, the hearse was flanked by 200 vaqueros, riding quarter horses wearing the famous *"Flying W"* brand. and later each rider circled her open grave before she was laid to rest at the Chamberlain Cemetery in Kingsville, Texas. [161]

Although the name of Richard King is known far and wide, Henrietta King never stood in his shadow. She was a fiercely independent and incredibly resilient woman. While Richard King operated the Santa Gertrudis Ranch of almost 32 years, Henrietta King operated the Ranch for another 40 years and virtually doubled its size. The legacy of Henrietta King extends far beyond the boundaries of the Santa Gertrudis Ranch. Her philanthropy was beyond compare. She represents the countless women who played crucial roles in shaping the frontier of Texas. Her life was a testament to the power of adaptability, the importance of family, and the enduring strength of the human spirit. She was a woman of quiet dignity, whose contributions to the heritage and history of Texas deserve to be celebrated.

Elizabeth "Lizzie" Johnson Williams
(1840 - 1924)

Elizabeth Johnson Williams
Creator Unknown
Image is in the Public Domain

Lizzie Johnson Williams, a name mentioned with a mix of awe and perhaps a touch of bewilderment, carved a remarkable path through the rugged landscape of the Texas frontier. The daughter of educators, Lizzie Johnson Williams, was destined to shatter expectations and redefine what a woman could achieve. Not content with the prescribed roles of wife and mother, she yearned for the thrill of the cattle drive and the satisfaction of building an empire. Through sheer grit, sharp intellect, and a spirit as untamed as the wild mustangs that roamed the prairies, she rose to become the "*Cattle Queen of Texas*."

Elizabeth Ellen Johnson was born on May 9, 1840, in Jefferson City, Missouri, to Thomas Jefferson and Catherine Hyde Johnson. She was the second of seven children in her family. Her mother was a music teacher, while her father taught a variety of subjects. In 1844, the family immigrated to the Republic of Texas, where Elizabeth's parents took up teaching positions in Huntsville, Lockhart, and Webberville.[162]

In 1852, her father established a private secondary school in Hayes County called the Johnson Institute. This co-educational boarding school initially consisted of log structures, some of which were built with the help of students. As the Institute expanded, Thomas Johnson hired additional teachers. After earning a degree from Chappell Hill Female College in 1859, Elizabeth (Lizzie) began teaching bookkeeping, French, mathematics, music, and spelling at the school. Thomas Johnson was a devout Methodist but invited preachers of different denominations to hold services at the Institute. In 1868, the Johnson Institute had 200 students and added a two-story, ten-room limestone structure, which served as a boardinghouse and school headquarters. Thomas Jefferson Johnson died on September 2, 1868, and was buried on the school grounds. After his death, his family continued to operate the school until 1872.[163]

Lizzie Johnson left the Institute long before its closing and held several teaching positions before opening her own primary school. Lizzie was never afraid of work, nor was she shy of ambition. She began doing bookkeeping on the side for additional income. As the business grew, some of her clients were successful cattlemen such as Major George Washington Littlefield, William H. Day, and Charles W. Whitis. Major Littlefield was especially impressed by Lizzie's drive and ability and remained close friends with her for the rest of his life. Being aware of the enormous profits that these cattlemen were making, Lizzie decided that instead of being an accountant for a cattle company, she wanted to own one.

Realizing that she did not have enough money to make her cattle ranch dream come true, she started writing short stories under a pen name and sold them to various newspapers and magazines, one of which was Frank Leslie's Illustrated Newspaper in New York. Because she wrote anonymously, No one knows exactly how many stories Lizzie actually wrote, but the financial games from them must have been substantial. She supposedly invested $2,500 in a cattle company in Chicago and sold her stock 3 years later for $20,000.

On June 1, 1871, Lizzie registered her cattle brand, an intricate "CY," which became number forty-five in the Travis County Clerk's Office registry. Two days later, she purchased 10 acres of land from Charles Whitis for $3,000 in gold. Initially, Lizzie's herd was too small for a trail drive, so she took advantage of the opportunity to round up some of the thousands of cattle roaming freely across the Texas landscape. She instructed her cowboys to round them up and place her brand on them, a procedure commonly known as "Brush Popping." Lizzie continued to invest in land and cattle, and soon she had enough to take to the market and travel the Chisholm Trail. Between 1871 and 1884, Lizzie drove several herds to market. While she was not the first woman to lead a trail drive to Kansas, she was the first to do so with cattle bearing her own brand. Similarly, she was not the first woman to wear the crown of "Cattle Queen," but it fit well when she wore it.

At age 39, Lizzie married Hezekiah George Williams on June 9, 1879. Little is known about Hezekiah ("Hez") other than he was born to Willam R. and Zerelda Johnson Williams in Montgomery County, Texas, on February 14, 1840, and that he was a widower with 7 children. Although the 1870 United

States Census for Guadalupe County, Texas, showed his occupation as *"Cattle Driver,"* he was said to be a former preacher. It appears that the only thing that Hez and Lizzie had in common was being born in the same year. Hez had little, if there was any, education and was a common cattle rancher who often made poor business decisions and was known to drink alcohol. In contrast, Lizzie was a refined, well-educated, highly skilled businesswoman who believed in temperance. Despite the differences in their character, the couple appeared to love each other.

Lizzie treated her marriage in the same way as a business relationship. Hez willingly signed a premarital contract that allowed her to retain all assets that she had acquired before the marriage and any assets that she acquired during the marriage. The couple kept all money and cattle separated. Hez even registered his own brand, but occasionally, Lizzie or Hez might ask the ranch hands to use their brand on one of the other's newborn calves without their knowledge.[164]

Lizzie's ambition didn't diminish after her marriage; if anything, it seemed to intensify. She continued to strategically expand her holdings in both cattle and real estate. She played an active role in the demanding work of driving her cattle to market. While Hez and the other cattle drivers rode horses, Lizzie opted for the relative comfort and practicality of a buggy. By the late 1880s, the era of the cattle drive was drawing to an end. Railroads were being built across the frontier, and an increasing number of landowners were fencing their property with barbed wire. However, Lizzie had successfully amassed a considerable fortune before the end of the cattle drives. This increased wealth allowed her and Hez the freedom to travel extensively. They stayed in the finest hotels everywhere they went, and Lizzie gave way to her refined tastes, seeking out the most exquisite dresses she could find. She also shopped for diamonds, not simply because of their aesthetic value, but because Lizzie viewed these precious stones as shrewd investments.

Just after the turn of the century, Cuba became a market for Texas cattle. Lizzie and Hez moved there for about three years. As it turned out, the market was not that lucrative. During their stay in Cuba, Hez was kidnapped by bandits. Lizzie quickly paid the $50,000 ransom that the bandits were demanding for Hez's safe return. Afterwords, Lizzie notified Hez the he owed her $50,000. [165]

Lizzie and Hez returned to Texas Christmas Eve, 1905. After arriving home, Hez was determined to establish a town in Hays County, Texas, which he named Hays City. It was located about 11 miles northwest of San Marcos. Lizzie was very supportive of his efforts, and the townsite did make some progress. When the Hays County Courthouse in San Marcos burned, on February 28, 1908, Hays petitioned the County for an election to move the County Seat to Hays City, but his petition failed. At one time, the community had a two-story hotel, one general store, a stable, a lumberyard, a church, and a weekly newspaper, but it was never able to attract enough settlers to support the town or acquire a post office. [166]

Brueggerhoff Building, Austin, Texas
creator unknown
Image is in the Public Domain

In all appearances, Lizzie and Hez enjoyed a happy marriage. Not so much into cattle anymore, Lizzie continued to buy land and buildings, including purchasing the Brueggerhoff Building at 919 Congress Avenue in downtown Austin. In her later years, Lizzie lived in an apartment there. The couple continued to travel even after Hez's health began to fail. Hez signed all of his assets over to Lizzie before his death.

While on a trip with Lizzie in El Paso, Hez died in July 1914. Lizzie purchased an elaborate casket for Hez's body to be transported back to Austin. It was said the paid $600 and wrote on the funeral home's bill: "*I loved this old buzzard this much.*" Hezekiah Williams was buried in Oakwood Cemetery, Austin, Texas on July 26, 1914. [167]

Lizzie outlived Hez by just over a decade, but she was a changed woman. She no longer wore her hair in her normal fashion and dressed so poorly that many of the people around her assumed that she was homeless. She lived out her final days in a small apartment of the building that she owned and still managed. Elizabeth Ellen Johnson "Lizzie" Williams died in Austin, Texas, on October 9, 1924, and was buried beside Hezekiah in Oakwood Cemetery. She left no will behind, and her heirs were forced to sort through the complicated affairs of her estate. An account from one of her nieces told that she found stashes of cash all over her apartment and found her diamonds in the basement of a building that she owned on 6th Street in Austin. Her heirs were shocked to discover that the net worth of her estate was almost $250,000 and that Lizzie owned land in Hays, Travis, Llano, Trinity, Culberson, Jeff Davis, and Montgomery Counties.[168]

From frontier schoolteacher to Texas Cattle Queen, Lizzie Johnson Williams defied the conventions of her time. Born in Missouri and raised in Texas, Lizzie's early life was steeped in education, resulting in her own teaching career. However, her ambition extended beyond the classroom. She established herself in the booming cattle industry and applied her exceptional business skills to build a successful cattle and real estate empire. Her marriage to Hezekiah Williams was marked by both affection and unusual financial arrangements, lasting for thirty-five years. Lizzie Johnson Williams was a true pioneer and a testament to the strength, courage, and ambition of early Texas women. Hers was a life well lived, and her story is one for the ages.

Mary Ann "Molly" Dyer Goodnight
(1839 - 1926)

Mary Ann Dyer Goodnight
by Swartz Cottage Gallery
courtesy of
Panhandle Plains Historical Museum
Image is in the Public Domain

The name Mary Ann "*Molly*" Dyer Goodnight is well known in the narrative of the Texas frontier, not only as the wife of a prominent cattleman but as a dynamic and influential force in her own right. Her achievements in establishing a ranching empire, advocating for animal welfare, and championing education reveal a woman of exceptional strength, compassion, and vision. Her story goes beyond the traditional narrative of a pioneer wife, showing a woman who made her own way and left her own mark on the history and heritage of Texas.

Mary Ann Dyer was born in Madison County, Tennessee, to Joel Henry and Susan Miller Dyer on September 12, 1839. She was the fourth in a large family of nine children. Her family moved to Fort Belknap, Texas, in 1854, where her father, Joel, established his law practice. In January 1856, Joel Dyer petitioned the State of Texas for relief benefiting Elizabeth Patton Crockett, David Crockett's widow. The petition was approved, granting her one league of land along with an additional 320 acres at the site of her residence.[169]

Fort Belknap was one of several forts in North Texas that formed a line separating current settlers from the western frontier, which was dominated by Native American Tribes. In the 1850s, it was a community of about 150 people, with several stores, and a couple of blacksmith shops. It also had a church, a school, a saloon, and a hotel. Because it was on the edge of the frontier, it became a staging point for cattle drives in the 1860s.

Mary Ann (Molly) had no formal education but had been taught by her parents, who were well-educated. By 1860, Molly was a teacher at Fort Belknap. During the War Between the States, several of her brothers joined the Confederate Army, and her brother Albert enlisted in Colonel J. E. McCord's Frontier Regiment. In late 1863, Molly met Charles Goodnight, a former Texas Ranger and Frontier Regiment veteran stationed at Fort Belknap. It was said that Charles was quite smitten by the attractive young school teacher. Molly and Charles lost contact with each other when Molly's family moved to Weatherford, Texas, in 1864, where Molly continued teaching. Molly's mother died in 1864, and her father died in 1866, leaving her to care for her younger brothers.[170]

In June 1866, Molly's former love interest, Charles Goodnight, partnered with Oliver Loving to drive a herd of cattle from Fort Belknap to Fort Sumner, New Mexico. Charles hired Molly's brother, Albert, to be a trail hand on the drive, beginning a lifelong friendship that lasted until Albert's death in 1911. Charles knew that one of the keys to a successful cattle drive would be the ability to feed all the cattle drivers along the trail. He bought an army surplus wagon manufactured by the H. & C. Studebaker Company and converted it into a rolling kitchen, which would carry all of the supplies and cookware necessary to prepare meals for his hungry cowboys. Charles named the massive wagon in his honor, calling it the "*Chuckwagon.*"[171]

The path of which soon would be known as the "*Goodnight-Loving Trail*" ran southwest along the old Butterfield Overland Mail route in Fort Belknap to the Horse Head crossing of Pecos River and then turned north along the west side of the river toward Fort Sumner. On their first trip, Goodnight and Loving delivered 2,000 head of cattle and returned to Texas with $12,000 in Gold.

In the summer of 1867, Charles and Oliver were on their third cattle drive to New Mexico when the herd was attacked by Comanches along the Pecos River. Despite Charles Goodnight's pleading, Oliver Loving decided to proceed in advance of the herd to finalize the sale. Shortly before reaching Fort Sumner, Loving and his scout, Bill Wilson, were attacked by Indians; while they both escaped, Loving received a severe wound in his arm, and after reaching Fort Sumter, the arm had gangrened and needed to be amputated. Charles Goodnight arrived while Loving was on his deathbed. Oliver asked Charles to take his body back to Texas after he died. Charles promised that he would, and Oliver Loving died at Fort Sumner on September 25, 1867, and was placed in a temporary grave while Charles Goodnight completed the cattle drive to Colorado.[172]

After returning to New Mexico, Charles hand Oliver Loving's body exhumed and carried it back to Weatherford, Texas for burial. He divided his profits from the cattle drive with the heirs of Oliver Loving. [173]

On a cattle drive through Colorado in 1869, Charles stopped and admired the prairie lands near Pueblo and decided it would be a perfect place for a ranch. He purchased a one-third interest in the 500,000-acre Nolan Land Grant and established his Rock Canyon Ranch there that same year. [174]

Charles returned to Texas in 1870 and renewed his romance with Molly Dyer. Molly and Charles were married on July 26, 1870, at the home of Nathan P. Harness, in Hickman, Fulton County, Kentucky. The couple spent their honeymoon in Colorado, where they stayed in a hotel in Pueblo until their home at the Rock Canyon Ranch was completed.

A story was told that on her first full day in Pueblo, she witnessed a vigilante mob hang three men from a telegraph pole. Wondering what kind of place her husband had put her in, Molley asked what he thought about it. Charles, trying to find a quick response to console his new wife replied, "*Well, I don't think it hurt the telegraph pole.*" [175]

Soon, the couple moved to her new home at the ranch, where they spent their first six years together. Molly's brother Albert lived at the ranch with them. A beautiful stone barn built by the ranch hands still stands today and is on the National Register of Historic Places. During the first three years of operation, the Rock Canyon Ranch showed a sizable profit, and Charles started investing in the town of Pueblo. Charles was a co-founder of the Stock Growers Bank of Pueblo, and he invested in the local opera house and a meat-packing facility at Las Animas.

In 1873, the fortunes of Charles Goodnight and the Rock Canyon Ranch took a turn for the worse. Severe weather, drought, overstocked ranges, and the panic of 1873 all took their toll. In addition, Molly wanted to return to Texas. After William Jackson Palmer bought the ranch, Charles sold all his other holdings in the area. In the fall of 1875, he moved 1,600 head of longhorn cattle to a place on the upper Canadian River in New Mexico and camped for the winter. Charles rode into Texas, scouting for a new place to move the cattle, and decided that Palo Duro Canyon in the Texas Panhandle would be the best location.

In 1876, Charles drove his cattle from the winter camp in New Mexico east to Tecovas Springs, then southeast to the Prairie Dog Town Fork of the Red River in Palo Duro Canyon. After establishing his new ranch, he returned to Colorado to borrow money and prepare to bring his wife back to her new home in Texas. While in Colorado in 1877, Charles met John George Adair, an English aristocrat who owned a brokerage company in Denver. Adair agreed to loan Charles money and showed an interest in the cattle business. Charles offered to partner with Adair in his ranch. Reluctant to buy land that he had never seen, Adair agreed to ride back to Texas with Charles.

In May 1877, Charles and Molly Goodnight, John Adair and his wife Cornelia, and four cowboys arrived at the ranch in Texas. On June 18, 1877, Charles Goodnight and John Adair drew up a five-year contract, with two-thirds of the property and profits going to Adair and one-third to Goodnight plus an annual salary of $2,500. At Goodnight's suggestion, the ranch was named with Adair's initials, J A. By the time their contract expired in 1882, the enterprise had realized more than $512,000 in profits, so the contract was extended for another five years. At the time of John Adair's death in 1885, the JA Ranch had reached 1,325,000 acres and was grazing more than 100,000 head of cattle.[176]

Although her nearest neighbor was miles away, Molly Goodnight was living a happy life. Along with the grueling chores of a pioneer wife, she was a doctor, spiritual advisor, sister, mother, and friend to all the ranch hands. They lovingly called her "*Aunt Molly*" because she was always mending their clothes, trying to educate them, and bringing them food. They once pooled their money and bought her a silver tea service.[177]

Perhaps the most endearing quality of Molly Goodnight was her genuine compassion. After spending sleepless nights listening to the lonely bleating of orphaned buffalo calves, she decided that something had to be done to prevent the buffalo from becoming extinct. She demanded that Charles and the cowboys round up the calves and bring them to her. The next day, Charles brought her two calves, and her brother brought her three. She bottle-fed them and treated them as if they were her children. Soon, even neighbors brought her orphaned calves, and her herd kept growing, so Charles set aside 600 acres for the care of the buffalo. At one point, the herd had grown to over 200, and some buffalo were shipped to other parts of the country. Descendants of this herd now live in the Caprock Canyons State Park. When DNA testing became available, it was discovered that the "*Southern Plains Buffalo*" were unlike buffalo from other parts of the country and that buffalo in the Goodnight herd were the last surviving members of the breed. Had it not been for Molly Goodnight, the breed would have vanished forever.[178]

Charles Goodnight sold his interest in the JA Ranch in 1987 and bought 160 sections (102,400 acres) in Armstrong County. He built a large two-story ranch house that he and Molly moved into on December 27, 1887. In 1898, Charles and Molly established Goodnight College, which operated until 1917.[179]

Mary Ann "*Molly*" Dyer Goodnight died at her home on April 11, 1926. She was buried in the Goodnight Cemetery. Engraved on her headstone are the words: "*One who spent her whole life in the service of others.*"

There is no greater testament to the strength and courage of early Texas women, than that of Molly Goodnight. Despite enduring years of isolation on an unforgiving frontier, she embraced her life there with passion and resilience. Loved and respected by everyone who crossed her path, her legacy has left an indelible mark on the Texas frontier that continues to inspire us today.

Anna Mebus Martin
(1843 - 1925)

Anna Mebus Martin
Creator unknown
Image is in the Public Domain

Brought to the frontier of Texas by immigrant parents seeking a better life, Anna Mebus Martin overcame poverty to become one of the wealthiest women in early Texas. Forced to assume the responsibility of supporting her family after her husband's crippling disease, Anna demonstrated her keen business skills by establishing a successful mercantile business, thriving cattle and real estate empire, and becoming the first woman bank founder and president in Texas.

Anna Jane Henriette Mebus was born in Germany to Alwill and Sophia Henriette Martin Mebus on December 10, 1843, and was the eldest of six children. When her father's business in Germany failed in 1858, he was lured by the promise of prosperity in Texas, where his wife's family resided. The Mebus family set sail from Germany on September 24, 1858, arriving at Galveston, Texas on December 7, 1858. After making the long journey to the Texas hill country, the Mebus family settled in a community called Hedwigs Hill, in Mason County, Texas, where Anna's uncle, Louis (Hedwig) Martin, was engaging in farming and ranching.

Mason County was in the heart of Comanche Territory, and while being a part of the Fisher-Miller Land Grant, given to German settlers in 1842, many were reluctant to settle there. Two major threats hindered new settlements in the area. The first and most prominent threat was repeated Comanche raids, which were most prevalent on nights with a full moon, causing settlers to refer to the occasion as "*the Comanche Moon*." The second major threat was attacks and looting by outlaws. Although Fort Mason had been established there in 1851, it did little to deter lawless activity in the area. Federal troops abandoned The fort on March 29, 1861, making the situation much worse.[180]

In December 1859, sixteen-year-old Anna Mebus married her cousin, Charles Karl Martin, who operated a store at Hedwigs Hill. Their marriage produced two sons. Charles Louis "*Karl*" Martin was born on October 14, 1861, and Max Martin was born on December 17, 1863.

Charles was appointed postmaster for Hedwigs Hill on August 21, 1861. Until 1861, Charles had a fairly successful business, but with the start of the War Between the States, his political views became his downfall. He was a staunch Republican and opposed secession, which was a dangerous philosophy in the Confederate State of Texas. Many of the locals stopped doing business with him, and his store was often damaged or looted, so he was forced to close down. Tragically, Charles was struck with inflammatory rheumatism in 1864, leaving him an invalid until his death in 1879.

After Charles became ill, Anna was forced to take responsibility for handling the family finances. She borrowed $150 and bought supplies and groceries to restock and reopen the store. Being in the path of the San Antonio-El Paso Mail line, Anna established a stagecoach stop. She boarded the horses, sold groceries to travelers, made butter, sewed, and handled the mail. After Anna earned a small supply of capital, she added dry goods to her stock and sometimes exchanged them for cattle. She began hauling freight and buying cotton and wool from local farms and ranches for sale in other areas. In the mid-1870s, cattle rustling became a significant problem, and Anna started selling barbed wire to ranchers who wanted to protect their herd. She sold more barbed wire than any company in West Texas. [181]

By the turn of the century, Anna owned more than 50,000 acres in Mason, Llano, and Gillespie counties and was the wealthiest German citizen in Texas. The local ranchers trusted her and began to pay her commissions for selling their livestock. At one time virtually every cattle transaction in Mason County was made through or with the approval of Anna Martin. [182]

In 1897, Anna sold her store and moved to Mason, Texas. Along with her two sons, Anna formed a partnership with Alfred Vander Strucken, W.J Moore, and T.J. Moore to establish the Commercial Bank of Mason on July 1, 1901. Anna was the bank's first president and held that position until 1925. The bank was owned by the Martin family until 1958 when her grandson Walter George Max Martin sold it shortly before his death. [183]

Anna Jane Henriette Mebus Martin spoke only German and French when she first came to Texas, and with no formal education, she had to learn English on her own. She was 73 years old when she became a United States Citizen on October 23, 1918. She died in Mason, Texas, on July 10, 1925, and was buried in the Martin Family Cemetery near the Llano River in Mason County, Texas.

As just a teenager, Anna Mebus Martin arrived in the hostile frontier of Texas just as it was on the brink of a civil war. Confronted with relentless attacks from the Comanches and outlaws, alongside the burden of her husband's crippling illness, Anna summoned extraordinary strength and courage to support her family in their most desperate moments. Despite her limited formal education and challenges stemming from language barriers, Anna transformed a modest country store into a booming enterprise. She skillfully leveraged the mail route and expanded into freight hauling, cattle trading, and real estate, earning the deep respect and trust of her fellow ranchers with her unwavering honesty. Defying gender bias, Anna claimed her place in history as the first woman bank president in Texas. Her remarkable story continues to inspire and remains a shining example of the strength and courage displayed by women of early Texas.

Charlotte Tompkins Thurmond "Lottie Deno"
(1844 ? - 1934)

Lottie Deno
Creator unknown
Image is in the Public Domain

Lottie Deno is a name well-known in the history of Texas and the history of the American West. While her legend is often larger than life, her image is one that paints the picture that most people see when imagining women in the old west. Styling herself as a Southern Belle, she wittingly adopted the persona of a gambler and saloon girl while disguising the truth about her shrewd business skills. She was more than a "painted lady" and used her limited options to forge her own destiny. Lottie Deno challenged the expectations of society and dealt herself a winning hand.

Charlotte Tompkins Thurmond, if in fact that is her correct name, was not born in Texas, nor did she die in Texas, but her life was a thesis statement for the story of the Texas frontier. We know very few facts about her life before coming to Texas. Lottie Deno became a part of Texas frontier folklore when her character was introduced in the 1909 historical fiction "*The Quirt and the Spur: Vanishing Shadows of the Texas Frontier*" by Edgar Rye. It has been said that the well-known character "*Miss Kitty*" in the long-running television series "*Gunsmoke*" was inspired by the life of Lottie Deno.

The only account of Charlotte's early life comes from her meeting with historian and author J. Marvin Hunter after the turn of the 20th century.[184] She recounted that she was born near Warsaw in Gallatin County, Kentucky, on April 21, 1844. Her father was a wealthy plantation owner who also raised and raced horses. He joined the Confederate Army and died during the war.

During the conflict, the Tompkins family lost their fortune, prompting Charlotte's mother to relocate with her and her sister to live with relatives in Detroit, Michigan. While in Detroit, Charlotte learned to gamble. After her mother's death, she began gambling on riverboats, traveling along the Mississippi River with her father's former jockey, Johnny Golden.

In 1865, Charlotte and Johny traveled from New Orleans to Texas along with her father's former slave, Mary Poindexter. In San Antonio, Charlotte started gambling at a saloon known as the University Club, owned by three brothers, Frank, Bob, and Harrison Thurmond. At some point, Frank Thurmond and Charlotte fell in love. Although they separated for a while, it was a romance that neither would forget. Over time, Charlotte started gambling at clubs all over San Antonio. She won so often that she acquired the nickname "*Queen of San Antonio.*" Another patron, amazed at her winnings, suggested that she change her name to "*Lotta Dinero.*"

Looking for more action, Charlotte made plans to move to Fort Concho in Tom Green County. Mary Poindexter made many friends while she was in San Antonia and decided to stay, so Charlotte made the trip alone. Women were in short supply in Fort Concho, and Charlotte made quite an impression when she arrived. Revealing nothing about her past, Charlotte continued her winning ways. Intrigued by her charm, one newspaperman gave her the nickname "*Mystic Maud,*" a name she kept during her entire stay at Fort Concho.

Sometime after 1869, Charlotte started traveling around Texas, using her newly adapted name, "*Lottie Deno.*" A woman of rare beauty on the frontier, Lottie drew attention everywhere she traveled. After visiting San Angelo, Denison, and Fort Worth, she traveled to Jacksboro, where she was charged with two counts of keeping a disorderly house, a charge typically associated with brothels.

Lottie settled at Fort Griffin in 1876. During her nearly three years there, Lottie bought 3 city lots and co-owned a saloon called "*The Gus.*" The town of Fort Griffin was known for being "*The Toughest Town in Texas*" and was described as "*one of the wildest gambling hellholes ever spawned on the frontier.*" In its glory days, the town had at least 18 saloons and more than its share of "soiled doves." The actual fort was built on a hill, but the town was located in the bottom land near the Clear Fork of the Brazos River, which was called "*The Flat.*"

The legend of Lottie Deno is synonymous with "*The Flat.*" Some of her acquaintances, such as Doc Holiday, Wyatt Earp, and Bat Masterson, were also legendary. One of her many stories involved a confrontation with Mary

160

Katherine Cummings (aka Big Nose Kate), the common-law wife of Doc Holiday. According to the story, in a fit of rage, Kate accused Lottie of having romantic affections for her man, and after a lengthy exchange of words, both women drew guns and had to be separated by Dock Holiday.

In January 1878, Lottie was charged with managing a brothel and ordered to stand trial. After being found guilty of the charge, Lottie filed an appeal but left town before the case came to trial. While wandering through Texas, she ran across her former lover, Frank Thurmond. The couple moved to New Mexico, where they continued to operate gambling parlors. Frank and Lottie were married in Silver City, New Mexico, on December 2, 1880. A short time later, they gave up their gambling enterprise and moved to Deming, New Mexico, where they lived the rest of their lives. Frank Thurmond died of cancer in 1908, and Lottie died on February 9, 1934. They are both buried in the Mountain View Cemetery in Deming, Luna County, New Mexico.

The legend of Lottie Deno has undoubtedly cast a more powerful influence on the history and culture of the Texas frontier than the reality of her life ever could. The vivid image of a flashy dressing, gun-slinging Southern belle who enchanted every cowboy in the gambling halls is what continues to define the Texas frontier for many. While the details of her true identity and actions may fade into obscurity, it is her captivating story that lives on, a timeless emblem of the vibrant and adventurous spirit of the Texas frontier.

The Preservationists

Texas, with its unique and vibrant history, owes much of its rich heritage to the tireless efforts of its women. While men often dominated the narratives of frontier life and political battles, women of early Texas quietly but powerfully preserved the stories, artifacts, and traditions that define the Lone Star State. From the pens of writers like Mary Austin Holley, chronicling early Texan experiences, to the passionate advocacy of women like Adina De Zavala and Clara Driscoll, fighting to protect historic landmarks, these remarkable figures shaped how Texas remembers its past. They ensured that the spirit and history of Texas would endure for generations to come.

Many of the unique and extraordinary women in early Texas, like Mary Ann Maverick, Susanna Dickinson, Juana Navarro Alsbury, and Maria Navarro, not only preserved the history but watched the events with their own eyes. Countless others have not received just recognition for their years of dedicated service through organizations such as the Daughters of the Republic of Texas, Daughters of the American Revolution, and United Daughters of the Confederacy. While their names have not been long remembered, their gift to the heritage and history of Texas is priceless.

Cornelia Branch Stone
(1840 – 1925)

Cornelia Branch Stone 1908
Creator unknown
Image is in the Public Domain

Born in the Republic of Texas, Cornelia Branch Stone passionately embraced the rich heritage given to her. Inspired by a father who fought for Texas independence and a mother who was the adopted daughter of one of the most prominent families in Texas, she devoted much of her life to preserving the history of the Lone Star State and those men and women who made it great. Her unwavering commitment and exemplary leadership serve as testaments to the true spirit of Texas.

Cornelia Branch was born at the home of Thomas Jefferson and Mary Frances Rusk on February 13, 1840. Her parents, Anne Cleveland Wharton and Edward Thomas Branch were married at the Eagle Island Plantation in Brazoria County, Texas. The elegant plantation was the home of Anne's adoptive parents, William Harris and Sarah Ann Groce Wharton.

Cornelia's father, Edward Thomas Branch, was an early resident of Liberty County, arriving at Anahuac in 1835. During the Texas Revolution, Edward served as First Sergeant in Captain William M. Logan's Company, Third Infantry, Second Regiment, Texas volunteers and fought at the Battle of San Jacinto. Edward Branch represented Liberty County in the First and Second Congress of the Republic of Texas and later was elected by Congress as Judge of the Fifth Judicial District, making him a member of the Texas Supreme Court. While serving as Judge, Edward and his wife Anne lived in the home of Thomas Rusk in Nacogdoches, where Cornelia was born in 1840.[185]

Cornelia's mother, Anne, was adopted at the age of ten by William and Sarah Ann Wharton after her mother died on the trip from New Orleans to Velasco, Texas, in 1833. She was raised in the luxury of the Eagle Island Plantation in Brazoria County. Anne's step-brother, John Austin Wharton, later became a

165

General in the Confederate Army, commanding the famed 8th Texas Cavalry, Terry's Texas Rangers. At the age of 42, Anne was heartbroken by the news that John Austin Wharton had been shot to death by one of his own men in 1865.

The Branch family returned to Liberty in the early 1840s. At the age of 15, Cornelia married Henry Clay Stone on April 16, 1856. The 27-year-old Henry was a farmer and a cotton broker. They welcomed their first child, a son named Branch Stone, on July 10, 1861; however, he tragically lived only 10 days. Cornelia faced further sorrow when her father passed away on September 24, 1861, at the young age of 49. On October 31, 1863, Cornelia gave birth to a daughter named Lena Stone, but heartbreak struck again when Lena died at the age of 2 on July 8, 1866. The one person who had been Cornelia's pillar of strength throughout her many devastating losses, her mother Anne, also passed away on January 27, 1867.[186]

Life expectancy in nineteenth-century Texas was short, and many of the women of early Texas experienced the pain of losing a loving parent at an early age. Even more tragically, many knew the pain of burying a child. Over time, the land where those loved ones rested became sacred. Protecting that land and preserving the memory of those who were so much a part of a rich heritage became a priority for some, and certainly, Cornelia Branch Stone was one who was passionate about the task.

On April 30, 1872, Cornelia Stone gave birth to a son, Harry Branch Stone, her only child who lived to adulthood. The care and education of her son became a priority to Carnelia.

Cornelia's uncle, Charles Lander Cleveland, lived in Liberty County for more than 25 years and was married to Mary Ann Hardin, daughter of one of the early settlers in Liberty. During his time in Liberty County, he was a lawyer, State Representative, and judge of the First Judicial District until he was removed by Radical Republican forces during Reconstruction. In 1871, Charles moved to Galveston, where he became a Federal Judge and was heavily involved in the banking, insurance, and cotton business. Because of his involvement in the cotton business, the Stone family moved there in 1877, where they lived prosperous lives for a decade. While on a trip to Austin, Texas, Henry Stone became ill and died suddenly in December 1887.

His body was transported to Liberty, Texas, where he was buried in the Branch Family Cemetery. After the funeral, Cornelia and her son Harry returned to Galveston and later toured England and Ireland, returning in September 1889. When Harry went to school to become a doctor, Cornelia lived in the Galveston home of her sister Olive and her husband George Briggs. From that point on, she devoted herself to the preservation of Texas heritage and the men and women who were a part of the glorious history.[187]

In 1891, Cornelia became involved with a group of women calling themselves the Daughters of Female Descendants of the Heroes of '36, which shortly after changed to Daughters of the Lone Star Republic. Their first meeting was held at the Houston home of Mary Jane Briscoe in November 1891, and at their first annual meeting in April 1892, they adopted the name Daughters of the Republic of Texas. Cornelia served two terms as the organization's second vice president and was involved in the effort to preserve the Alamo.

Over the next decade, Cornelia was involved with the Daughters of the American Revolution, Colonial Dames, Confederated Southern Memorial Association, and United Daughters of the Confederacy. Her most dedicated service was to the United Daughters of the Confederacy (UDC). She was twice president of the Texas Division of the UDC, and, in 1908, was elected President-General of the UDC national organization. Historian Karen Cox noted that the President-General of the UDC was "*one of the most powerful political positions a southern woman could hold in the late nineteenth and early twentieth centuries.*"[188]

In March 1906, the UDC made plans to place a Confederate Memorial at the Arlington National Cemetery. Cornelia Stone became the first president of the Arlington Confederate Memorial Association in 1907. The Association was responsible for supervising the design and construction of the Memorial. The renowned sculptor and former Confederate soldier Moses Jacob Ezekiel was commissioned to create the Memorial in November 1910. Due in part to the fund-raising efforts of Cornelia Stone, the Memorial was unveiled by President Woodrow Wilson on June 4, 1914. Cornelia's pivotal role in placing the Monument at Arlington National Cemetery was likely her most satisfying accomplishment. Honoring those who gave so much to Texas and to the

South was a big part of her life. Although posthumously, that moment was taken from her when a wave of perceived political correctness forced the Monument to be removed on December 20, 2023.

Confederate Memorial, Arlington National Cemetery 1914, Library of Congress, Image is in the Public Doman

Although she once served as Vice-President of the Texas State Historical Association, Cornelia's devotion to service did not stop with the preservation of history. She was an active member of the Democratic Party and worked diligently for election reform. She was also an advocate for women's rights and served as first vice president of the Texas Federation of Women's Clubs and two terms as president of the Texas Woman's Press Association. She was also a board member of the Texas Fine Arts Association and board of trustees of the Rosenberg Library of Galveston.[189]

Cornelia Branch Stone spent her final years at the home of her nephew, Clay Stone Briggs, a U.S. Congressman from Texas. She died in Washington, D. C. on January 18, 1925. Her body was first taken to Galveston, Texas, where a ceremony was held at the home of Congressman Briggs. Her casket was draped by a Confederate Flag as family, friends, and members of the United Daughters of the Confederacy, Daughters of the American Revolution, and Daughters of the Republic of Texas said their final goodbyes. She was then taken to Liberty, Texas, and buried in the Branch Family Cemetery.

Born into a family with deep ties to the Republic of Texas, she experienced both the hardships and triumphs of early Texan life. Despite facing profound personal losses, she found the strength and courage to serve and honor her loved ones. She became a key figure in numerous historical and patriotic organizations. Cornelia's story highlights the significant role that women played in shaping historical narratives during a crucial period in Texas and American history. Her contributions to the preservation of Texas history and heritage will be remembered for years to come.

Adina Emilia De Zavala
(1861 – 1955)

Adina Emilia De Zavala
Creator unknown
Image is in the Public Domain

The granddaughter of a signer of the Texas Declaration of Independence and the first vice-president of the Republic of Texas, Adina de Zavala developed a passion for preserving history at an early age. Her story is one of fierce dedication and her name should be etched alongside the heroes of the Alamo, not for fighting and dying there, but for wielding the weapon of unwavering conviction in preserving one of the Lone Star State's most sacred shrines.

Adina De Zavala was born in Harris County, Texas, on November 28, 1861. She was the first child born to Augustine and Julia Tyrrell De Zavala. Her mother was Irish, and her father was of Mexican and Anglo descent.

Adina's grandfather was Lorenzo de Zavala, who signed the Texas Declaration of Independence and was the first vice-president of the Republic of Texas. Lorenzo resigned his position as Mexican Minister to France and moved to Texas in July 1835, where he bought property on the north shore of Buffalo Bayou across from what would be the site of the Battle of San Jacinto. He died from complications of pneumonia on November 15, 1836, and was buried on his property. Family members continued to be buried there in the family cemetery until the early 20th century. After the family moved from the property, the cemetery was transferred to the State of Texas, but by the early 1960s, much of the cemetery was underwater due to erosion and subsidence. The State of Texas relocated the cemetery to the San Jacinto Battleground State Historic Site in 1970, but because no coffins or human remains were found, only the remaining grave markers were transferred.[190]

Adina's family moved to Galveston shortly after the Confederate Army drove Union forces off the island in 1863. She attended the Ursuline Academy at Galveston from 1871 to 1873 when the family moved to San Antonio. Adina enrolled at Sam Houston Normal Institute at Huntsville in 1879 (now Sam

Houston State University) and graduated there in 1881. She attended a school of music in Missouri for a short time before becoming a teacher in Terrell, Texas, in 1884. Adina returned to San Antonio in about 1887 and was teaching there when she began meeting with a group of women interested in preserving Texas history. Adina joined the Daughters of the Republic of Texas (DRT) organization in 1893 and quickly became very active.[191]

The State of Texas purchased the Alamo Chapel from the Catholic Church in 1883, but the wholesale grocery firm Hugo and Schmeltzer Company still owned the mission convent, also known as the Long Barrack. Being a devoted historian, Adina realized the critical role played by the long barrack during the siege, and prior to joining the DRT, she had obtained a verbal promise from the grocery firm to give her a first chance at buying the property.

In 1903, Clara Driscoll joined the DRT and became Adina's friend. The following year, Clara used her personal funds to purchase the long barrack from the Hugo and Schmeltzer Company. The State of Texas later purchased the property from Driscoll and gave custody of the Alamo to the DRT in January 1905.

Soon, a dispute arose within the DRT over procedures for preserving the Alamo, with one faction supporting Clara Driscoll and the other supporting Adina De Zavala. The Driscoll faction was under the mistaken belief that the Hugo and Schmeltzer Company building was built after the siege and wanted to demolish the dilapidated building. Adina insisted that the long barrack played a more pivotal role in the battle than Alamo Chapel. She waged a protest to prevent its destruction, and in February 1908, she barricaded herself inside the long barrack for 3 days. Eventually, the courts ruled in favor of Clara Driscoll, but Adina was able to preserve portions of the original wall of the convent.

In addition to her work with the DRT, Adina was a member of numerous organizations, including the United Daughters of the Confederacy, Texas Folklore Society, Philosophical Society of Texas, and Texas Woman's Press Association. She organized the Texas Historical and Landmarks Association in 1912, placing thirty-eight markers at historic sites in the State, and promoted the preservation of the Spanish Governor's Palace in San Antonio. With the Texas State Historical Association, Adina was a charter member, a member of the executive council beginning in 1919, and was elected honorary life fellow of the Association in 1945. She was appointed to the Texas Historical Board in 1923 by Governor Pat Neff and was one of the original members of the Committee of One Hundred appointed to plan for a state centennial. Adina was also on the advisory board of the Texas Centennial Committee. A gifted writer, she had many published works including her book, "*History and Legends of the Alamo and Other Missions in and Around San Antonio.*"[192]

Adina was never married but was always a devoted daughter, sister, and Catholic. Her incredible life ended on March 1, 1955, at the age of 93. She was buried in the family plot at Saint Mary's Cemetery in San Antonio, Texas.

Though the battles over brick and mortar raged, her true victory was in the enduring spirit she ignited. She was not merely preserving a shrine but safeguarding the very soul of Texas. With every marker placed, every story told, she wove herself into the tapestry of her beloved state. Time may erode monuments, but it could never diminish the fire she kindled. Adina proved that history is not just a collection of dates and names. In the heart of Texas, her spirit remains a beacon that illuminates a glorious past.

Clara Driscoll
(1881 – 1945)

A woman with a deep love for history, Clara Driscoll was a true Texas patriot. Descending from Irish immigrants who cherished the heritage of early Texas, she utilized all her resources to navigate the complex political landscape and ensured that the Alamo would be preserved for future generations. Without her relentless commitment and visionary leadership, the site of this iconic battle could have been lost to time.

Clara Driscoll was born in St. Mary's of Aransas, Texas on April 2, 1881. The town was once a thriving community in Refugio, County and for a short time served as the County Seat. Her parents were Robert and Julia Fox Driscoll, and Clara's paternal grandfather was Daniel O'Driscoll, an Irish immigrant.

Daniel O' Driscoll had been serving in the U. S. Army at Fort Jessup, Louisiana, until he decided to immigrate to Mexican Texas in 1835, and join the Texas Revolution. As a sergeant in Captain Andrew Briscoe's Company, he fought at the Battle of San Jacinto. After the battle, Daniel continued serving in the Texas Army and was appointed second lieutenant on January 15, 1837. In Victoria, Texas in December 1837, he married Catherine Magrath Duggan, a widow whose husband Patrick, died in route from New Orleans to Refugio. The couple was living in Refugio County when their son Jeremiah was born in 1838, and when their son Robert was born in 1841. Daniel was murdered in 1849, and after his wife Catherine died in 1852, Jeremiah and Robert were raised by their half-sister, Ellen Duggan Doughty. When Texas seceded from the Union in 1861, Jeremiah and Robert joined the Confederate Army. Clara's father, Robert, served in Company K, 21st Texas Cavalry. After the war, the two brothers moved to St. Mary's of Aransas and soon owned cattle and land in Refugio, Victoria and Bee counties.[193]

Robert Driscoll married Julia Fox on December 27, 1870, and their first child, Robert, Jr., was born on October 31, 1871. Their daughter, Clara, was born almost ten years later. At the time of Clara's birth, Robert Driscoll was on the verge of establishing a cattle empire. In 1884, Robert bought the 83,000-acre Palo Alto Ranch, and moved his family there. By 1890, he had become a multi-millionaire and was invested in cattle, real estate, and banking. A man with endless resources, Robert and Julia enrolled their daughter, Clara in private schools in Texas, New York, and France.[194]

Clara returned to Texas at the age of eighteen and became interested in Texas history. As her parents and grandparents had been citizens of the Republic of Texas, she joined the Daughters of the Republic of Texas in 1903. Clara and her friend Adina De Zavala were appalled by the deterioration of the 3-acre plaza of the Alamo plaza, especially the old convent known as the Long Barrack.

Although the State of Texas had previously purchased the Alamo chapel in 1883, the Long Barrack was owned by Hugo and Schmeltzer Company. When the property was placed up for sale the asking price was $75,000 and was purchased by the Daughters of the Republic Texas. The vast majority of the money was paid by Clara Driscoll personally. After the Texas State Legislature authorized a $65,000 payment to Clara, she conveyed title of the property to the State of Texas on October 4, 1905, the State then named the DRT as custodians for both the Alamo chapel and Long Barrack. Soon after being designated custodians of the Alamo, a dispute arose over the management of the grounds.[195]

Mistakenly believing that the Long Barrack was built after the battle, Clara and a group of followers decided that the badly deteriorating Long Barrack needed to be demolished. The plan was bitterly opposed by Adina De Zavala and her followers. After years of litigation, and protest, the courts ruled in favor of the Driscoll faction but a portion of the wall of the convent was preserved.

While lobbying the State of Texas, Clara met Henry Hulme (Hal) Sevier, a Texas House Representative from Uvalde County. Hal moved to New York in 1906, and later married Clara on July 31, at St. Patrick's Cathedral.[196]

After Clara's father died in 1914, she and Hal returned to Austin to be near her family's financial interests. Hal established a daily newspaper, the Austin American, and Clara served as president of the Daughters of the Republic of

Texas. Clara bought a 14-acre site, once owned by Stephen F. Austin, on Mount Bonnell overlooking Lake Austin. She had a Mediterranean-style villa built on the property in 1916, and named it Laguna Gloria.

After Clara's brother, Robert Driscoll, Jr., died in 1929, she and Hal moved to her family's Palo Alto Ranch in order to manage her newly inherited empire of petroleum and land and serve as president of the Corpus Christi Bank and Trust Company. She continued to devote herself to public service and the preservation Texas history. She liquidated all the debts of Texas Federation of Women's Clubs, donated her elegant Laguna Gloria villa to the Texas Fine Arts Association, and became vice-chairman of the Texas Centennial Exposition.[197]

In 1837, her thirty-one-year marriage to Hal Sevier ended in divorce and she resumed her name as Clara Driscoll. In 1942, to honor her deceased brother, she built the 20-story Robert Driscoll Hotel in Corpus Christi and was living in a high-rise penthouse apartment there when she died suddenly of a cerebral hemorrhage on July 17, 1945. After her body ceremonially laid in state in the Alamo Chapel, she was buried at the Masonic Cemetery in San Antonio, Texas. The bulk of her 7-million-dollar estate was bequeathed to the building and maintenance of the Driscoll Foundation Children's Hospital in Corpus Christi.

From her remarkable contributions to the preservation of the Alamo to her extensive philanthropic efforts, Clara Driscoll was a pivotal figure in Texas history. She harnessed her influence to shape the narrative of the state, demonstrating an unwavering commitment to its heritage. Her enduring legacy is not just a testament to her passion, but a powerful reminder of the lasting impact one woman can have on the spirit of Texas.

Bibliography

Comanche Moon Falling
Drew McGunn - CreateSpace Independent Publishing - 2018

Houston Madam: The Story of Pamelia Mann, Texas Pioneer
Gene Shelton - CreateSpace Independent Publishing - 2016

Indian Depredations in Texas
J. W. Wilbarger - Coyote Texts - 2019

Jane Long Mother of Texas
Catherine Troxell Gonzalez - Eakin Press - 1981

Memoirs of Mary A. Maverick: A Journal of Early Texas
Mary A. Maverick - Maverick Publishing Company - 2005

Outlaws in petticoats and other notorious Texas women
Ann Ruff and Gail Drago - Republic of Texas Press - 1995

Sunshine on the Prairie
Jack C. Ramsey - Eakin Press - 1990

The Story Of Lottie Deno: Her Life And Times
J. Marvin Hunter - Kessinger Publishing - 2007

Texas Tales: Stories That Shaped a Landscape and a People
Myra Hargrave McIlvain - Sunstone Press - 2017

Texas Tears and Texas Sunshine, Voices of Frontier Women
Jo Ella Powell Exley - Texas A & M Press - 1985

Notes

[1] *"Texas Day by Day"*, Handbook of Texas Online, Texas State Historical Association, https://www.tshaonline.org/texas-day-by-day/entry/28

[2] Russell, Amber, *"Social Structure of the Spanish Colonies,"* Smithsonian Learning Lab, Smithsonian

[3] Hendricks, Rick, *"Corpus Christi de la Isleta Mission,"* Handbook of Texas, Texas State Historical Association, https://www.tshaonline.org/handbook/entries/corpus-christi-de-la-isleta-mission.

[4] Weddle, Robert S., *"San Francisco de los Tejas Mission,"* Handbook of Texas, Texas State Historical Association, https://www.tshaonline.org/handbook/entries/san-francisco-de-los-tejas-mission

[5] Galan, Francis X., *"Los Adeas, the first capital of Spanish Texas,"* College Station: Texas A & M University Press, p. Introduction

[6] https://www.tshaonline.org/handbook/entries/san-francisco-de-los-tejas-mission

[7] https://www.tshaonline.org/handbook/entries/angelina

[8] https://www.tshaonline.org/handbook/entries/bellisle-francois-simars-de

[9] https://tpwmagazine.com/archive/2012/jun/LLL_angelina/

[10] https://www.charmeasttexas.com/features/finding-angelina-the-search-for-east-texas-little-angel/article_0967770a-3374-11ec-bab5-0f783e71385f.html

[11] Roe, Russell, *"Pinewoods Pocahontas,"* Texas Parks and Wildlife Magazine Online, https://tpwmagazine.com/archive/2012/jun/LLL_angelina/

[12] Henson, Margaret Swett. *"Long, Jane Herbert Wilkinson"*. Handbook of Texas Online. Texas State Historical Association, https://www.tshaonline.org/handbook/entries/long-jane-herbert-wilkinson

[13] Mississippi, U.S., Compiled Marriages, 1800-1825 Mississippi, U.S., Compiled Marriages, 1800-1825

[14] Headstone, Morton Cemetery, Richmond, Texas.

[15] Treaty of Amity, Settlement and Limits between the United States of America, and His Catholic Majesty, February 22, 1821

[16] Warren, Harris Gaylord, *"Long Expedition,"* Handbook of Texas Online, Texas State Historical Association. https://www.tshaonline.org/handbook/entries/long-expedition

[17] Henson, Margaret S., *"Long, Jane Herbert Wilkinson (1798–1880)."* Handbook of Texas Online, Texas State Historical Association, https://www.tshaonline.org/handbook/entries/long-jane-herbert-wilkinson

[18] Hardin, Elizabeth J. E., *"Kian,"* Handbook of Texas Online, Texas State Historical Association, https://www.tshaonline.org/handbook/entries/kian

[19] Henson, Margaret S., *"Long, Jane Herbert Wilkinson (1798–1880)."* Handbook of Texas Online, Texas State Historical Association, https://www.tshaonline.org/handbook/entries/long-jane-herbert-wilkinson

[20] Warren, Harris Gaylord, *"Long Expedition,"* Handbook of Texas Online, Texas State Historical Association. https://www.tshaonline.org/handbook/entries/long-expedition

181

[21] Henson, Margaret S., *"Long, Jane Herbert Wilkinson (1798–1880)."* Handbook of Texas Online, Texas State Historical Association, https://www.tshaonline.org/handbook/entries/long-jane-herbert-wilkinson

[22] Ibid.

[23] Austin's Colony Records (SC.AC). Archives and Records Program, Texas General Land Office, Austin.

[24] Henson, Margaret S., *"Long, Jane Herbert Wilkinson (1798–1880)."* Handbook of Texas Online, Texas State Historical Association, https://www.tshaonline.org/handbook/entries/long-jane-herbert-wilkinson

[25] Bertleth, Rosa Groce, *"Jared Ellison Groce*," Texas State Historical Association, The Southwestern Historical Quarterly, Vol. 20, No. 4 (April 1917), pp. 358-368

[26] ibid

[27] Weir, Brian, *"Wharton, Sarah Ann Groce (1810–1878),"* Handbook of Texas Online, Texas State Historical Society, https://www.tshaonline.org/handbook/entries/wharton-sarah-ann-groce

[28] Combined Works, *"Houston, a history and guide"* Bureau of research in social sciences of the University of Texas. Sponsored by the Harris County Historical Society, Inc., Anson Jones Press, Houston, Texas, 1942. https://archive.org/stream/houstonahistory00writmiss/houstonahistory00writmiss_djvu.txt

[29] McIlvain, Myra Hargrave: *"Texas Tales: Stories That Shaped a Landscape and a People,"* Sunstone Press, Santa Fe, New Mexico (April 1, 2017).

[30] Stephen F. Austin's Register of Families, volume 1.

[31] Roll of Wm. J. E. Heard's Company F, 1st Regiment, Texan Volunteers, Colonel Edward Burleson Command.

[32] McArthur, Judith N., *"Hallett, Margaret Leatherbury,"* Handbook of Texas Online, Texas State Historical Association. https://www.tshaonline.org/handbook/entries/hallett-margaret-leatherbury

[33] ibid

[34] ibid

[35] Lavaca County TXGenWeb Project, Hallett Cemetery/Hallettsville City Memorial Park, http://www.lavacacountyhistory.org/cemeteries_h_k.htm

[36] Texas, Select County Marriage Index, 1837-1965

[37] *Bugbee, Lester G. "The Old Three Hundred,"* The Quarterly of the Texas State Historical Association, (October 1897), 108-117

[38] Texas Historical Commission Marker Number 12787, erected 2002 near Eagle Lake, Wharton County, Texas.

[39] Texas, Select County Marriage Index, 1837-1977, Colorado County, Texas.

[40] Texas, County Marriages, 1817-1965, Colorado County, Texas 20 Mar 1843.

[41] Texas, County Marriages, 1817-1965, Banquet, Nueces County, Texas 17 Oct 1852

[42] DeWitt Colony Land Grants 1825-1832from the files of the General Land Office of the State of Texas

[43] https://www.thealamo.org/remember/battle-and-revolution/defenders/almaron-dickinson

[44] Historical marker erected by the State of Texas, 1936, County Road 197 and South St. Joseph Street (U.S. 183), Gonzales, Texas

[45] Morphis, James M. "*Susanna Hanning (Dickinson) Interview.*" History of Texas, from its discovery and settlement page 176. New York: United States Publishing Co., 1874.

[46] Texas, Select County Marriage Index, 1837-1965

[47] 1850 U. S. Federal Census, Houston, Harris County, Texas.

[48] Texas Historical Commission marker, number 9776. 308 West San Antonio Street, Lockhart TX

[49] Texas, Select County Marriage Index, 1837-1965, Caldwell County, Texas

[50] Burleson, Georgia J., "*The life and writings of Rufus C. Burleson*," 1901 page 741

[51] Missouri, Marriage Records, 1805-2002, Marion County, Missouri

[52] Muir, Andrew Forest, "*Mexican Border Ballads and Other Lore.*" University of North Texas Press, 1946.

[53] https://www.findagrave.com/memorial/189677042/marshall-mann

[54] Muir, Andrew Forest, "*Mexican Border Ballads and Other Lore.*" University of North Texas Press, 1946.

[55] https://www.findagrave.com/memorial/189200141/tandy_k_brown

[56] https://www.findagrave.com/memorial/189199845/pamelia_brown

[57] Historical marker placed by the Louisiana Society Daughters of the American Revolution at 2nd St #200, Natchitoches LA

[58] https://www.sonsofdewittcolony.org/trudeaumadame.htm

[59] McArthur, Judith N., Texas State Historical Association, Handbook of Texas Online, https://www.tshaonline.org/handbook/entries/wright-margaret-theresa-robertson

[60] ibid

[61] ibid

[62] Historical Marker: Margaret Wright "*The Mother of Texas*" placed by the City of Victoria

[63] Brown, John Henry, "*Indian wars and pioneers of Texas,*" [Austin: L.E. Daniel, 1890]

[64] ibid

[65] ibid

[66] ibid

[67] Ragsdale, Crstal Sasse, "*Kleberg, Robert Justus II (1803–1888),*" Handbook of Texas History Online, Texas State Historical Association, https://www.tshaonline.org/handbook/entries/kleberg-robert-justus-i

[68] ibid

[69] van Kleef, Alisa, "*Robert Justus Kleberg II (1853-1932),*" Immigrant Entrepreneurship: German-American Business Biographies, 1720 to the Present. German Historical Institute, Washington, DC., http://www.immigrantentrepreneurship.org.

[70] Tennessee Marriages to 1825, Sumner County

[71] Texas State Library and Archives Commission, *"Republic of Texas - The Archives War,"* https://www.tsl.texas.gov/treasures/republic/archwar/archwar.html

[72] McClear, Sheila, *"The Fascinating Story of the Texas Archives War of 1842,"* Smithsonian Magazine, October 9, 2018. https://www.smithsonianmag.com/history/fascinating-story-texas-archives-war-1842-180970470/

[73] Alamo Trust, Inc., *"Independence and Annexation,"* https://www.thealamo.org/remember/military-occupation/independence-and-annexation

[74] Indiana, Marriages, 1810-2001, Allen County, Jesse A. Aughinbaugh and Sophia Suttenfield

[75] Maguire, Jack, *"Sophia Porter, Texas' Own Scarlet O'Hara,"* included in the book by Abernethy, Francis Edward, *"Legendary Ladies of Texas,"* University of North Texas Press; Denton, Texas (July 1, 1994)

[76] ibid

[77] Grayson County TXGenWeb, https://usgenwebsites.org/TXGrayson/Crime&Punishment/Felony/Galloway_CharlesA.html

[78] Maguire, Jack, *"Sophia Porter, Texas' Own Scarlet O'Hara,"* included in the book by Abernethy, Francis Edward, *"Legendary Ladies of Texas,"* University of North Texas Press; Denton, Texas (July 1, 1994)

[79] Texas, U.S., County Marriage Records, 1817-1965, James Porter - Sophia Butt, McLennan County, Texas

[80] Maguire, Jack, *"Sophia Porter, Texas' Own Scarlet O'Hara,"* included in the book by Abernethy, Francis Edward, *"Legendary Ladies of Texas,"* University of North Texas Press; Denton, Texas (July 1, 1994)

[81] ibid

[82] ibid

[83] Fort Parker Massacre, https://en.wikipedia.org/wiki/Fort_Parker_massacre

[84] Plummer, Rachel, *"The Rachel Plummer Narrative,"* Forgotten Books, Dalton House, London, 1926

[85] Exley, Jo Ella Powel, *"Rachel Parker Plummer,"* *Texas Tears and Texas Sunshine*, Texas A & M Press, College Station, TX, 1985.

[86] ibid

[87] Ramsey, Jack C. Jr., *"Sunshine on the Prairie,"* Eaton Press, Fort Worth, TX, 1990

[88] Wilbarger, J. W., *"Indian Depredations in Texas,"* Independently published, J. W. Wilbarger, 2019

[89] ibid

[90] Hacker, Margaret Schmidt, *"Parker, Cynthia Ann (ca. 1825–ca. 1871),"* Handbook of Texas Online, Texas State Historical Association, https://www.tshaonline.org/handbook/entries/parker-cynthia-ann

[91] *The Galveston Daily News.* (Galveston, Tex.), Vol. 35, No. 126, Ed. 1 Friday, June 4, 1875, Page: 2.

[92] Maverick, Mary Ann, *"Memoirs of Mary Ann Maverick,"* Alamo Printing Company, San Antonio, Texas, 1921.

[93] Schilz, Jodye Lynn Dickson, *"Council House Fight,"* Handbook of Texas History Online, Texas State Historical Association, https://www.tshaonline.org/handbook/entries/council-house-fight

[94] Maverick, Mary Ann, "*Memoirs of Mary Ann Maverick*," Alamo Printing Company, San Antonio, Texas, 1921.

[95] ibid

[96] ibid

[97] Fenstermaker, Anne Leslie, "*Maverick, Samuel, Jr. (1837–1936)*," Handbook of Texas History Online, Texas State Historical Association, https://www.tshaonline.org/handbook/entries/maverick-samuel-jr

[98] Maverick, Mary Ann, "*Memoirs of Mary Ann Maverick*," Alamo Printing Company, San Antonio, Texas, 1921.

[99] Marks, Paula Mitchell, "*Maverick, Samuel Augustus (1803–1870)*," Handbook of Texas History Online, Texas State Historical Association, https://www.tshaonline.org/handbook/entries/maverick-samuel-augustus

[100] Fisher, Lewis F., "*St. Mark's Episcopal Church*," Handbook of Texas History Online, Texas State Historical Association, https://www.tshaonline.org/handbook/entries/st-marks-episcopal-church

[101] Horton, Margaret Ann, Dallas County Pioneer Association, https://dallaspioneer.org/pioneers/enoch-horton-and-martha-stinson-horton/

[102] Jones, Barney C., Dallas County Pioneer Association, https://dallaspioneer.org/pioneers/alexander-cockrell-and-sarah-horton-cockrell/

[103] ibid

[104] ibid

[105] ibid

[106] City of Dallas, Dallas Landmark, Structures and Sites, American Beauty Mill. https://dallascityhall.com/departments/sustainabledevelopment/historicpreservation/Pages/american_beauty_mill.aspx

[107] Enstam, Elizabeth York, "*Cockrell, Sarah Horton (1819–1892)*," Handbook of Texas History Online, Texas State Historical Association, https://www.tshaonline.org/handbook/entries/cockrell-sarah-horton

[108] Ritchey, David, "*Holekamp, Betty Wilhelmine Abbenthern (1826–1902)*," Handbook of Texas History Online, Texas State Historical Association, https://www.tshaonline.org/handbook/entries/holekamp-betty-wilhelmine-abbenthern

[109] ibid

[110] ibid

[111] Brister, Louis E., "*Adelsverein*," Handbook of Texas History Online, Texas State Historical Association, https://www.tshaonline.org/handbook/entries/adelsverein

[112] Ritchey, David, "*Holekamp, Betty Wilhelmine Abbenthern (1826–1902)*," Handbook of Texas History Online, Texas State Historical Association, https://www.tshaonline.org/handbook/entries/holekamp-betty-wilhelmine-abbenthern

[113] "*Battle of the Nueces*," Handbook of Texas History Online, Texas State Historical Association, https://www.tshaonline.org/handbook/entries/nueces-battle-of-the

[114] United States National Archives, US, Civil War Service Records, Confederate, Texas.

[115] 1860 United State Federal Census Rolls, Kendall County, Texas

[116] 1870 United State Federal Census Rolls, Kendall County, Texas

[117] 1880 United State Federal Census Rolls, Kendall County, Texas

[118] 1900 United State Federal Census Rolls, Kendall County, Texas

[119] Hughes, Marie, *"Sarah Ridge ~ Displaced by Manifest Destiny,"* Chambers County Museum at Wallisville, https://wallisvillemuseum.com/footprints-sarah-rdge

[120] Ladd, Kevin, *"Pix, Sarah Ridge (1814–1891),"* Handbook of Texas History Online, Texas State Historical Association, https://www.tshaonline.org/handbook/entries/pix-sarah-ridge

[121] ibid

[122] findagrave.com, *"Emily Anderson "Oo-loo-stah" Paschal,"* https://www.findagrave.com/memorial/119334384/emily_anderson_paschal

[123] findagrave.com, *"Susan Agnes "Soonie" Paschal,"* https://www.findagrave.com/memorial/9405749/susan_agnes_paschal

[124] findagrave.com, *"Emily Anderson "Oo-loo-stah" Paschal"* https://www.findagrave.com/memorial/119334384/emily_anderson_paschal

[125] findagrave.com, *"Ridge Watie Paschall,"* https://www.findagrave.com/memorial/6813054/ridge_watie_paschall

[126] findagrave.com, *"Susan Agnes "Soonie" Paschal,"* https://www.findagrave.com/memorial/9405749/susan_agnes_paschal

[127] findagrave.com, *"Emily Agnes Paschal McNeir,"* https://www.findagrave.com/memorial/9399100/emily_agnes_mcneir

[128] Hughes, Marie, *"Sarah Ridge ~ Displaced by Manifest Destiny,"* Chambers County Museum at Wallisville, https://wallisvillemuseum.com/footprints-sarah-rdge

[129] 1850 United States Census, Galveston, Galveston County, Texas

[130] Ladd, Kevin, *"Pix, Sarah Ridge (1814–1891),"* Handbook of Texas History Online, Texas State Historica Association, https://www.tshaonline.org/handbook/entries/pix-sarah-ridge

[131] 1850 United States Census, Galveston, Galveston County, Texas

[132] Hughes, Marie, *"Sarah Ridge ~ Displaced by Manifest Destiny,"* Chambers County Museum at Wallisville, https://wallisvillemuseum.com/footprints-sarah-rdge

[133] https://www.findagrave.com/memorial/56937360/george_walter_paschal

[134] findagrave.com, *"Ridge Watie Paschall,"* https://www.findagrave.com/memorial/6813054/ridge_watie_paschall

[135] Hughes, Marie, *"Sarah Ridge ~ Displaced by Manifest Destiny,"* Chambers County Museum at Wallisville, https://wallisvillemuseum.com/footprints-sarah-rdge

[136] ibid

[137] ibid

[138] Texas Land Title Abstracts, Grantee William H. Blair, Certificate 220, Patent #671, Volume 5.

[139] United States National Archives, US, Civil War Service Records, Confederate, Texas

[140] Wiedenfeld, Melissa G., *"Gay, Bettie Munn (1836–1921),"* Handbook of Texas History Online, Texas State Historical Association, https://www.tshaonline.org/handbook/entries/gay-bettie-munn

[141] ibid

[142] Long, Christopher, *"McMullen-McGloin Colony."* Handbook of Texas History Online, Texas State Historical Association, https://www.tshaonline.org/handbook/entries/mcmullen-mcgloin-colony

[143] Heffernan, Mary, *"The Heffernan Families"* A History of Bee County: With some brief sketches about men and events in adjourning counties.1939

[144] Texas Marriage Collection, 1814-1909 and 1966-2002, Milton H. Hardy/Margaret Dunbar, Victoria County, Texas

[145] 1860 United States Federal Census, Victoria, Texas

[146] McNutt, James C., *"Borland, Margaret Heffernan (1824–1873),"* Handbook of Texas History Online, Texas State Historical Association, https://www.tshaonline.org/handbook/entries/borland-margaret-heffernan

[147] Roell, Craig H, *"Rose, Victor Marion (1842–1893),"* Handbook of Texas History Online, Texas State Historical Association, https://www.tshaonline.org/handbook/entries/rose-victor-marion

[148] Curlee, Kendall, *"Peticolas, Alfred Brown (1838–1915),"* Handbook of Texas History Online, Texas State Historical Association, https://www.tshaonline.org/handbook/entries/peticolas-alfred-brown

[149] ibid

[150] McNutt, James C., *"Borland, Margaret Heffernan (1824–1873),"* Handbook of Texas History Online, Texas State Historical Association, https://www.tshaonline.org/handbook/entries/borland-margaret-heffernan

[151] Sneed, Edgar P, King, *"Henrietta Chamberlain (1832–1925),"* Handbook of Texas History Online, Texas State Historical Association, https://www.tshaonline.org/handbook/entries/king-henrietta-chamberlain

[152] Ehrlich, Allison, *"Influential Women of South Texas: Henrietta King,"* Corpus Christi Caller Times. March 31, 2020. https://www.caller.com/story/news/local/2020/03/31/influential-women-south-texas-henrietta-king/4830423002/

[153] ibid

[154] Cheeseman, Bruce S., *"King, Richard (1824–1885),"* Handbook of Texas History Online, Texas State Historical Association, https://www.tshaonline.org/handbook/entries/king-richard

[155] Sneed, Edgar P, King, *"Henrietta Chamberlain (1832–1925),"* Handbook of Texas History Online, Texas State Historical Association, https://www.tshaonline.org/handbook/entries/king-henrietta-chamberlain

[156] Cheeseman, Bruce S., *"King, Richard (1824–1885),"* Handbook of Texas History Online, Texas State Historical Association, https://www.tshaonline.org/handbook/entries/king-richard

[157] Barnhart, Don, *"The Mexico Connection,"* Warriors of the Lone Star Blogspot, posted April 29, 2012. https://warriorsofthelonestar.blogspot.com/2012/04/mexico-connection.html

[158] Cheeseman, Bruce S., *"King, Richard (1824–1885),"* Handbook of Texas History Online, Texas State Historical Association, https://www.tshaonline.org/handbook/entries/king-richard

[159] Vick, Francis B., *"Kleberg, Alice Gertrudis King (1862–1944),"* Handbook of Texas History Online, Texas State Historical Association, https://www.tshaonline.org/handbook/entries/kleberg-alice-gertrudis-king

[160] ibid

[161] Sneed, Edgar P, King, *"Henrietta Chamberlain (1832–1925),"* Handbook of Texas History Online, Texas State Historical Association, https://www.tshaonline.org/handbook/entries/king-henrietta-chamberlain

[162] Duncan, Roberta S., *"Williams, Elizabeth Ellen Johnson [Lizzie] (1840–1924),"* Handbook of Texas History Online, Texas State Historical Association, https://www.tshaonline.org/handbook/entries/williams-elizabeth-ellen-johnson-lizzie

[163] ibid

[164] James M. Smallwood, James M., *"Elizabeth (Lizzie) Johnson Williams,"* Texas Women on the Cattle Trails, Texas A & M Press, College Station, Texas, March 2019

[165] ibid

[166] Green, Daniel P., *"Hays City, TX,"* Handbook of Texas History Online, Texas State Historical Association, https://www.tshaonline.org/handbook/entries/hays-city-tx

[167] Chisholm Trail Heritage Center, 2150 Chisholm Trail Pkwy, Duncan, Oklahoma.https://www.facebook.com/onthechisholmtrail/videos/lizzie-johnson/1159029347823515/

[168] Duncan, Roberta S., *"Williams, Elizabeth Ellen Johnson [Lizzie] (1840–1924)*," Handbook of Texas History Online, Texas State Historical Association, https://www.tshaonline.org/handbook/entries/williams-elizabeth-ellen-johnson-lizzie

[169] Roach, Joyce Gibson, *"Goodnight, Mary Ann Dyer [Molly] (1839–1926),"* Handbook of Texas Histoy Online, Texas State Historical Association, https://www.tshaonline.org/handbook/entries/goodnight-mary-ann-dyer-molly

[170] ibid

[171] Anderson, Hugh Allen, *"Goodnight, Charles (1836–1929)*," Handbook of Texas Histoy Online, Texas State Historical Association, https://www.tshaonline.org/handbook/entries/goodnight-charles

[172] ibid

[173] ibid

[174] Schreck, Chris, *"Spoils of War: Development and Dispossession in the American Southwest,"* https://scalar.usc.edu/works/the-colorado-fuel-and-iron-company/pueblo-colorado

[175] Roach, Joyce Gibson, *"Goodnight, Mary Ann Dyer [Molly] (1839–1926)*," Handbook of Texas Histoy Online, Texas State Historical Association, https://www.tshaonline.org/handbook/entries/goodnight-mary-ann-dyer-molly

[176] Anderson, Hugh Allen, *"Goodnight, Charles (1836–1929),"* Handbook of Texas Histoy Online, Texas State Historical Association, https://www.tshaonline.org/handbook/entries/goodnight-charles

[177] Bone, Louie, *"The Mother of the Panhadle,"* Texas Parks and Wildlife Magazine, https://tpwmagazine.com/archive/2020/may/wildwomen/index.phtml

[178] Ibid

[179] Anderson, Hugh Allen, *"Goodnight, Charles (1836–1929),"* Handbook of Texas Histoỷ Online, Texas State Historical Association, https://www.tshaonline.org/handbook/entries/goodnight-charles

[180] Large, Deborah S., *"Martin, Anna Henriette Mebus (1843–1925),"* Handbook of Texas History Online, Texas State Historical Association, https://www.tshaonline.org/handbook/entries/martin-anna-henriette-mebus

[181] ibid

[182] ibid

[183] The Commercial Bank of Mason, https://www.tcbmason.com/about-us/bank-history

[184] Hunter, J. Marvin, *"The Story Of Lottie Deno: Her Life And Times,"* Kessinger Publishing (July 23, 2009)

[185] Banks, Ted, *"Stone, Cornelia Branch (1840–1925),"* Handbook of Texas History Online, Texas State Historical Association, https://www.tshaonline.org/handbook/entries/stone-cornelia-branch

[186] ibid

[187] ibid

[188] ibid

[189] ibid

[190] *"De Zavala Cemetery."* Texas Time Travel, Texas Historical Commission, https://texastimetravel.com/directory/de-zavala-cemetery-tour/

[191] Ables, L. Robert, *"Zavala, Adina Emilia De (1861–1955),"* Handbook of Texas History Online, Texas State Historical Association, https://www.tshaonline.org/handbook/entries/zavala-adina-emilia-de

[192] ibid

[193] Givens, Murphy, *"Clara Driscoll and the second battle of the Alamo,"* Corpus Christi Caller-Times, March 30, 2016.

[194] DeMoss, Dorothy D., *"Driscoll, Clara (1881–1945),"* Handbook of Texas History Online, Texas State Historical Association,https://www.tshaonline.org/handbook/entries/driscoll-clara

[195] Eckhardt, C. F., *"The Second battle of the Alamo,"* https://www.texianlegacy.com/eckhardt.html

[196] DeMoss, Dorothy D., *"Sevier, Henry Hulme (1878–1940),"* Handbook of Texas History Online, Texas State Historical https://www.tshaonline.org/handbook/entries/sevier-henry-hulme

[197] DeMoss, Dorothy D., *"Driscoll, Clara (1881–1945),"* Handbook of Texas History Online, Texas State Historical Association,https://www.tshaonline.org/handbook/entries/driscoll-clara